Writers Have No Age: Creative Writing With Older Adults

About the Authors

Lenore M. Coberly, Jeri McCormick, and Karen Updike are teachers of writing in Creative Arts Over 60, a program for older adults in Dane County, Wisconsin. Lenore and Jeri are co-editors of *Heartland Journal*, a magazine of writing by older authors. Karen Updike edited *Echoes from Mount and Plain,* an anthology of work by older adults from rural areas.

Lenore leads summer writing workshops at Green Lake School of the Arts. She is a published poet, book reviewer, and article writer. Jeri co-edited *Poetry Out of Wisconsin V,* 1980, and has edited a variety of state government publications. Karen's book of poems, *Sonja,* has been dramatized and produced.

Writers Have No Age: Creative Writing With Older Adults

Lenore M. Coberly
Jeri McCormick
Karen Updike

The Haworth Press
New York

Writers Have No Age: Creative Writing With Older Adults has also been published as *Activities, Adaptation & Aging,* Volume 6, Number 2, Winter 1984.

The Haworth Press, Inc., 28 East 22 Street, New York, New York 10010

Library of Congress Cataloging in Publication Data

Coberly, Lenore M.
  Writers have no age.

  "Has also been published as Activities, adaptation & aging, volume 6, number 2, winter 1984"—T.p. verso.
  Bibliography: p.
  1. English language—Rhetoric—Study and teaching. 2. Creative writing—Study and teaching. 3. Education of the aged. I. McCormick, Jeri. II. Updike, Karen. III. Title.
PE1404.C55 1984   808'.0420715   84-15715
ISBN 0-86656-320-2
ISBN 0-86656-351-2 (pbk.)

Writing has given me a reason to live . . .
besides, it keeps us off the streets.

—Wanda Hile
in her ninth decade

Writers Have No Age:
Creative Writing With Older Adults

Activities, Adaptation & Aging
Volume 6, Number 2

CONTENTS

Foreword

We have been given a gift and a guide.

I am pleased to present—in a manner of speaking—three talented writers who share their craft and offer ideas on how their experience can be useful to others. The authors of this book have, through years of valuable experience, discovered what it takes to spark the creative energy of older writers. They have been very mindful of what seemed to work and what didn't. Each has watched with all of the love and attention of a master teacher but also with the critical eye of a sensitive writer, to discover what it takes to encourage individuals who have, through their lives, been so engaged in other work that they have missed the joy that comes from writing clearly, shaping important ideas, and enjoying the craftsmanship of it.

This book is a gift. It is given from those who have clearly enjoyed the time they have invested to bring a group together. They have discovered and honed the talents of their students. They have helped to shape and appreciated their students' ideas and feelings. This book is a gift given to those of us eager to learn how to stimulate creativity among older persons.

This book is also a guide that offers to one concerned about the craft of writing practical counsel on how to help others discover within their own beings creative capacity and how to tap the wells of experience of older writers. As a guide, the book leads the reader through the steps that have proven helpful to these three writer-teachers so that their objective analysis of what worked and what didn't work could become a guide for another teacher. This book is indeed a guide for gifted, committed, dedicated teachers.

The book is also a guide for a growing number of individuals who have taken the time and invested the energy to bring together people—many for the first time in their lives—to think about what writing is and what it expresses and what it stores up as treasures for tomorrow. This book will prove invaluable to teacher-writers as they face new opportunities and perplexing dilemmas.

The first time through, simply accept the gift, the insights, the joys, the anecdotes, and appreciate the fact that accomplished writer-teachers thought enough of you to share their experience and what they have learned through the years.

The second time through, consider it a guide to your development of a course plan, a syllabus, an outline. As a guide, this book will take you through the geography of a good writing workshop, a classroom, a library. It will prove useful to you as you develop a course, a strategy, a style by which your skills, talents, and dedication can be brought effectively together for and with your students of all ages.

Keep it handy. You will find, as I have, numerous occasions when what the authors have shared will be immediately applicable and useful. Add it to your pens and paper, to your outlines and notes, to your diary and manuscripts. Keep it near your desk; take it to class with you.

Enjoy it as a gift; appreciate it as a guide; use it as a tool.

James T. Sykes
Vice-President
National Council on Aging

Preface

Writers Have No Age: Creative Writing With Older Adults is a guide for the teaching of creative writing in senior centers and nursing homes. The book identifies likely students and suitable teachers, and outlines appropriate procedures for starting and continuing writing classes. In addition to providing a framework and rationale for programming, the book features a set of detailed lesson plans and provides listings of lesson and teacher resources.

Thanks to Rosella Howe, who encouraged us to write this book, Marjorie Berlow, director, Creative Arts Over Sixty, and, above all, our students in many centers who have been our teachers. Our special thanks to those who have permitted us to use their work in this book.

Lenore M. Coberly
Jeri McCormick
Karen Updike

Photo by Brent Nicastro.

Introduction

Five years ago when we began teaching writing workshops for older adults in southwestern Wisconsin, we combed the library looking for a book such as this one. Though there were none, there were, of course, books on how to teach writing, books on older adult programs, and booklets of their work which had somehow been produced and collected under several different programs in the country. But there was no book telling how and why at the same time. So we floundered along at first, often using up our own poetry ideas as writing assignments, sharing with students our enthusiasm for the self-validating activity of writing even as we tried to establish and model the discipline and rewards in the life of a writer.

We are writers ourselves, writers who have taught in various capacities, but never writing as we are now practicing it, and certainly not to this special population. We think of writing as a way of sharing one's heart and mind with others, of teaching as a way of sharing our enthusiasm for that process, and this book as a reaching out to other writers who may wish to teach this unique group.

Older adults are potential writers possessed of rich lodes of experience to mine and the leisure and solitude for the work. More than we who are still employed in satisfying work, they crave the experience of wrestling with something, making something emerge from their vigorous effort. Why not wrestle with themselves, as they confronted and continue to confront their own lives? Writing class is a place to be heard and enjoyed weekly, a class that capitalizes on a lifetime of fine work as a proper subject for art. Writing allows older adults to continue to enjoy a sense of power and control over their lives, to retain the sense of being the acting agent instead of the acted upon, the constrained, constricted object of other people's attention or neglect. At a time when many seniors are relegated to the rocking chair, those fortunate enough to be involved in the arts can retain their sense of self.

In "A Nature Poem Written Indoors," John Stone writes "and you and I/ Having switched through bird from fish/ to this/ to hair from fur/ Little keeps us as we are./ We survive by what we were."

But we stop being really alive if we rest on our laurels and do not use the skills and experiences of the past to contend with our present. The alive person is always in a process of growing and evolving from one stage of relative protection and safety to another. In a poem he calls "An 80 Years Self, Portrait," Alex Stevens writes about how he still is having to change in order to preserve his sense of self: He declares that if he were a saint or a bird or a dog or a child, he would know what was going to happen to him, "But as I am I/ I am content to be what I am not content to stay;/ the husks untidier each spring . . . "

Writing is important to people of all ages because it preserves man's real inner self, his growing, changing, evolving self. Members of a recent writing workshop all said they felt writing had aided their general sense of well-being because it had "brought them back to themselves." In his "Essay on Sanity," Stephen Dunn writes "Nevertheless it is with our poems/ that we must visit ourselves, who are/ neither here/ nor there." Writing brings us news about ourselves, who we really are, what we can hope to be, just as surely as the Times or the Journal brings us news of the outer world. Saying that writing brings us back to ourselves suggests that we may have somehow lost ourselves along the way. We may have forgotten to listen to ourselves because we were so involved in taking care of others. We may not have had the courage to listen to ourselves and act upon the consequences of defying others. We may not have dared to let go of one way of being and face the uncharted land of a new way of being. We may have tried to pretend that we are other than we really are and not even have known that we were pretending. Not to feel that you are the one who acts is to feel dead, even if you are still alive. Kierkegaard tells us, "The greatest danger, that of losing one's own self, may pass off as if it were nothing; every other loss, that of an arm, a leg, five dollars, a wife, is sure to be noticed." Coming to know oneself and one's friends more truly through writing is the very reason for the humanities in general and literature in particular. Without the lubricating or leavening influence of art flowing through our lives, helping us to change ourselves, we do stop growing, we do lose ourselves.

Writing classes inject a sense of adventure in lives perhaps too "cabined, cribbed, confined," too tuned to the past as a source of pleasure and security. Herman Hesse knew he had idealized away the pain by painting a "green picture of my earliest life." Sheldon Kopp has called nostalgia a form of revenge. If one remains muddled in nostalgia, or if one insists on literally transcribing things as they say they really were, he misses the excitement of transforming experience into art. At first older adults will find common ground in similar memories—they have all walked the country road to school, smelled inkwells and sweeping compound or watched trolleys clank along their tracks. They write of the safe things with which all can easily identify. Gradually older writers will come to value not their similarities but their differences, each unique viewpoint, descriptive eye, narrative gift. Wonder of wonders, they are not all of a piece. From one they come to expect a poem, from another wit. One builds a reputation for insightful if bawdy depictions of river folk. Like the various people in *Our Town* who viewed the same spring moon with quite different reactions, the writers find that the past has meant different things to each. Soon they exchange their comfortable addiction to an idealized past for the tangible pleasure and artistic satisfaction of creating in the present a specific, vivid real past. Judith Leet writes, "Very encouraging: we all have locations, moments, and voices; and there is room for our individual versions of the world."

* * *

It is difficult
to get news from poems
yet men die miserably every day
for lack
of what is found there.

—William Carlos Williams

* * *

Paying attention to the past, re-inspecting it, or looking at it again (which is the origin of the word *respect:* to value something enough to want to look at it again, as opposed to not giving something a second glance) . . . re-inspecting the past teaches looking at the present with sharper, more accurate, observation. Re-inspecting the person we were in the past, when we flourished with the zest, spontaneity and autonomy characteristic of an untrammeled childhood, reminds us of that way of being again. It encourages us to preserve that way of being even as adults. Recreating the past self in stories, being alert to remembered sensual details and images that enliven our writing, helps us pay attention to strong hints from our unconscious as it guides and directs us to become, to preserve and to nurture our real inner selves. One woman said, "This class brings memories long forgotten." She was talking of more than memories, but was referring to things as yet undiscovered.

Thus we have seen that art, including writing, orders, inspires, and enables us. It orders the confusing, chaotic images and events of our amorphous, unstructured past and helps us perceive meaning in what is really random, unpredictable, and impersonal. It inspires us to realize in our present lives the positive, self-nurturing values we remember and recreate from our early selves. And it enables us to tap the fertile waters of our unconscious and live our lives as much as possible as our real selves, doing what we want to do, not what others want us to do, or society or family thinks we should do.

The activity of writing sets in motion the most gratifying relationships with oneself, with the class and friends, with one's family and ultimately with one's community. These interactions are far more important to the older writer than the sheets of paper he holds in his hand. Writing programs which seek to compile a picture of the twenties, or oral history programs which amass reams of tapes from speakers who never again hear the words they have spoken, are settling for too little. They are focusing on obtaining a product for themselves rather than providing the deepening and self-validating process of art for the older writer. In a poem about a whittling class, which might just as well be a writing class, John Stone urged the members: "Go ahead now/ May you find/ in the waiting wood/ rough unspoken/ what is true/or/ nearly true/ or/ true enough."

We should not be surprised that the process of writing is so energizing, so life-enhancing.

> It is almost like a religious experience to work with language because language creates form and order. The man who writes out of an inner need is trying to order his corner of the universe. You begin with the chaos of events and impressions and feelings, you marshall your arguments and metaphors, pound and hammer them into shape and form, feel the marvelous informing order emerge from it and feel reborn!

writes Maxine Kumin in *To Make A Prairie*. The older writers say among themselves, "It's better than bridge!"

Good writing for all of us is close to the well-spring. It comes up to us through the pipes of the unconscious, if we let it. It percolates through the ground of our being, refreshing us, rinsing away the arid encrustations of mask and role, our outer room, and restores us to our true selves. Gradually the students realize that writing class is where the language of strong feeling has an important place. It is a place to pay attention to the world and to our unconscious, a place to identify how we feel and what we want, a place to speak in a way that is real, if not polite, a place to celebrate new understandings.

We have put together some of our own best ideas and methods and rationales to help you bring the re-creation and stimulation of writing to people over sixty who probably thought that writing classes, for them, were surely a thing of the past.

Helen I. Klingelhofer kept customers in her beauty shop entertained with stories. Now she writes them. Photo courtesy of The Wisconsin State Journal.

Chapter 1

Who Are the Students?
The Diverse Motivations
That Attract Students
to Writing Classes

*We arrive out of many singular rooms, walking over the
branching streets.
We come to be assured that our brothers surround us,
to restore their images upon our eyes.
We enlarge our voices in common speaking and singing.
We try again that solitude found in the midst of those
who with us seek their hidden reckonings.*

—*Kenneth L. Patton*

In this poem Kenneth L. Patton was speaking of the reasons for
assemblies in houses of fellowship all over this land, but after experiencing more than five years of writing classes with older adults,
we realize that his words have particular application to writing
workshops as well.

As great a variety and diversity exists among older adults as in
those of other ages. Such will be the case with the students who arrive for writing class. But whatever the varied reasons for their
coming and the unique talents which they bear with them, they will
have in common the desire to be heard by others and the need to be
confirmed in themselves. For writing reminiscences, and ultimately
writing anything at all, is more than just an attempt to put the
chronological pieces of one's life together; it is a search for whole-
ness and health, a desire for unity of body, mind, and spirit through
exploring what it has meant and continues to mean to be oneself.

7

In his old age, Charles Darwin lamented that his mind had become a sort of sausage machine for grinding factual observations into scientific systems. He said that had he been able to live his life over again he would have frequently read poetry and listened to music because "the loss of these tastes is a loss of happiness, and may possibly be injurious to the intellect and more probably to the moral character."

—Clyde S. Kilby

* * *

In a lighter moment we composed a check list designed to ascertain whether or not the writing workshop was for the new entrant.

Is the Writing Workshop for You? Take This Twelve Point Check Up to Decide!

1. Do you like to write long letters to friends?
2. Have you ever spent a good amount of time practicing your signature or doodling flourishes on paper for pleasure?
3. Do you clip and save ideas and clever sayings from the newspaper or other reading material?
4. Do you remember with pleasure one or two special books you have read in your life?
5. Can you still recite a poem you were required to memorize in grade school?
6. Do some people seem to like to hear the special way you have of telling about an experience?
7. Do you count among your special friends people who have an interesting way of talking about things?
8. Do you privately think that you appreciate and notice the world of nature more than do your family and friends?
9. Can you see humor in situations others find irritating?
10. Do you want to feel a rush of energy and joy in your life as springtime fills the land?
11. Do you want to discover things about yourself you have not known before?
12. Do you want to be able to look at something longer than it lasts?

If you answer yes to 6 points or less, perhaps another workshop is for you.

If you answer yes to 8 or more, this workshop is your cup of tea.

If you answer yes to 10 or more, you have hidden talent!

If you answer yes to all 12, who is your publisher?

This list moves from concrete gratifications to the most elusive satisfactions to be found in the experience of writing; its game-show format was designed to propose lightly the pleasures of coming together with others to write. Mary Hedin in *The Writer* magazine (1 March 1982) declares she has yet to find a person who wants to write and thinks of doing so, who can't. Such confidence is heartening news indeed for those who walk tentatively through that door for the first time, bearing like heavy suitcases their doubts, reservations, and rationalizations about their talent and their real objectives for writing. Most contend they merely want the history of their family preserved. That seems the most acceptable and self-effacing motive for such high self-indulgence as attending the enrichment class we teach. Some actually come via geneological research projects. Others have always thought of themselves as writers, if they had only had the time to devote to it. Now that time has arrived. Some have whole drawers full of poems and short stories but have never had any feedback on them, opportunity to read them, or courage and know-how to go about marketing them.

Some have written in narrow technical areas such as library science or forestry and now want to write for a wider audience. They see writing as a natural extension of their earlier work, and the class as a chance to share both parts of themselves. Former social workers, teachers, worship service makers, newsletter editors, and English major-homemakers fit this category.

Some are such extroverts they just plain enjoy an audience and will write to obtain one. A few have led such stimulating and exciting lives, senior citizen activity other than the writing group now looks pale to them in comparison.

Once the class has started, recruits appear, some inappropriately and uncomfortably dragged along by enthusiastic class members, some thrust into your midst by well-meaning friends and family as "therapy." One such woman called a teacher's home to ask in a puzzled way, "Why do I have your number on a slip of paper by my phone?"

Those who come to keep the wife company or, conversely, to keep an eye on their husbands, and those who come because other classes are closed are usually misplaced, and drop out. There are however some who come purely for fellowship after a major loss, such as the recently widowed or newly retired, and only later come to know the genuine satisfactions of selecting and ordering experience in art.

Usually however, your most enthusiastic participants will be those older adults who have finally given themselves permission to develop another side of themselves, to be artistic. Perhaps they feel that since the body is announcing increasingly its physical limitations, they had best sharpen and focus the mind and imagination by writing things down and ordering them. They have a new freedom to ask, "What am I about? Am I anything without my work? Without my wife? Am I really just a social worker? Really just a housewife?" They know in their bones that retired from one life must not mean retired from all life. They are waiting to take up a new vocabulary in which they will discover things about themselves not known before, find a forum for that which cannot be said in their usual social conversations and delight in new fresh ways of speech. At some level they must hope that they will respond to an increased use of their senses with a heightened awareness of their own aliveness and love of the world, even as they age.

* * *

Youth is a gift of nature; age is a work of art.

—Anonymous

* * *

In the valediction at the end of his wonderful poem "The Universe Is Closed and Has REM's," George Starbuck states his reason for writing about the world he loves, a world "so beautiful, so varied, so new."

> I take it as my task to record
> at close hand, for the glory of no Lord,
> delight of no posterity, some part
> of what it was to take the world to heart

Chapter 2

Who Should Teach?
Attitudes and Skills
of Effective Teachers
With Older Adults

Thank you for guiding me through my formative years. . .

—Valentine greeting from an older student
to her creative writing teacher

SUCCESSFUL TEACHERS

Successful teachers usually measure success in terms of the growing independence of students. This independence can be the goal only to a point with older students.

They will become better and better writers, surprising with their growth, but ultimate independence is not what they are after. They know they are at that time in their lives when growing dependence is inevitable. They want as much independence as possible and they want your help in achieving and maintaining this, but the young student's expectation of achieving freedom from dependence is not for them. Time is moving the other way for the older student.

It follows that the successful teacher of older adults is in the business of encouraging and fostering all of the independence possible while remaining sensitive to the level of support needed. Finally this support is supplied in increasing amounts.

This is not to say that there will be no completely and fiercely independent older people in your classes who continue that way until the last second of life. There will be, but they are exceptional. The gracious and courageous acceptance of limitations is more likely to be the case. It is not easy to help those who need to be raised from self-pity to self-confidence, but focusing on writing and away from the rest of the individual is your best tool.

Teachers recognize that writing is serious work for Eliza Kavana and Hazel Boehm. Photo courtesy of Creative Arts Over Sixty.

Individuals we know who have worked successfully with creative writing classes with older adults are different in cultural and educational backgrounds from one another but they have both obvious and apparently unimportant similarities. At the outset, all were practicing free-lance writers available to teach part-time. All were published poets although their other writing experiences varied.

Older adults appear to enjoy a classroom structure with a teacher clearly in charge. This changes, however, if the teacher is rigid or careless of the time of the group. Careful preparation for class and meticulous attention to evaluating manuscripts implies a respect for the time and efforts of the participants, but this is not enough. As in any group, there are individuals who will demand more than their share of attention and others who will lose focus on the subject under discussion. Some elderly persons can be prevented from disrupting the group only by a self-confident and caring leader who can enlist the rest of the group in reassuring the troubled member.

A single group of older adults responding to an announcement of a creative writing class may include those with less than a high school education and some with advanced degrees. Retired academics and professional people often want to write for a broader audience or in a different field than when they were active in their professions. They often have a more difficult time getting started in creative writing than those who simply have the desire to write or who have been writing in secret. E. Michael Brady of the University of Hartford, in studying people who have attended Elderhostel programs, concluded that the less educated benefited more than the majority who had graduate degrees (AARP News Bulletin, July-August, 1983). This poses no problem for the teacher who is comfortable with a wide variety of educational levels. The members of the group will be comfortable together if the teacher is.

Class members and teachers who are writers are likely to be searching for a forum where they can talk about writing and where people will like them *because they are writers.* The importance of choosing teachers who are writers should not be overlooked. The new identity of members *as writers* is an important aspect of success. Writing imposes no age limitations and transcends physical limitations. The enthusiasm the teacher feels is contagious and one of the first surprises members new to writing discover is that they need never be bored. Grist for the writer's mill is everywhere—in a sickroom, at a shopping mall, on a bus, in the nest of a crow, or in a puddle on the street.

The beauty of art and the richness of poetry gives order, form and harmony, a kind of temporary limited perfection, to a frustrating ambiguous disinterested discontinuous unpredictable senseless world . . . Science, religion, politics, philosophy, math are all simply metaphoric ways of looking at the aimless on-going stream of life. Each perspective is no more than a reassuring hedge that lets us pretend that we might dam, direct, or at least chart the chaotic course of its current. No matter how elaborate, none serves as anymore than a tale told to ease our journey.

— *"An End to Innocence," Sheldon Kopp*

* * *

Among writers, as among any group of people, are those who have a strong need to serve others. To be able to fill that need and remain with writing is a delight for such persons. It seems obvious that a teacher must like people and have experience with groups, but enjoying older people is different from enjoying the young. They know *so much* and their motivation is ready-made, therefore the teacher must not be distracted from the subject of writing.

Laughter is such an important part of writing classes that it deserves serious attention. A teacher without a sense of humor is probably useless anywhere, but in these classes such a teacher would be a deficit as well. Patients at a county home would walk down the hall to stand near the class and hear the laughter, even if they did not participate in the class. Staff members at senior centers express envy of the writing groups because of the laughter they hear.

What is the source of this merriment? People are communicating with each other, and the human condition, honestly reported, is pretty sad and pretty funny. Both students and teacher must be able to see humor in small things as well as in the great.

* * *

Writers may not be special—sensitive or talented in any usual sense. They are simply engaged in sustained use of a language skill we all have. Their "creations" come about through confident reliance on stray impulses that will, with trust, find occasional patterns that are satisfying.

—*William Stafford*

One woman, assigned to visit the shopping mall and recount a conversation she overheard, wrote about hearing an older woman advocate the use of prune juice. She observed that the speaker wore a brown sweater with creases and that her face was brown with creases. She was a prune! A dull encounter had been turned into a good laugh.

At a nursing home there was an exciting air of expectancy as each person read what he had written about candy corn; despite all having written from the same assignment, each was different. One woman saw a single piece of the candy as an Indian tepee with white smoke coming out of the top. She ended her piece with the remark that she couldn't eat an Indian tepee, especially since she was diabetic. There it was, both humor and pathos, the stuff of writing.

A man who had been paralyzed for seven years wrote about traveling when he was a boy—from the back door to the outside toilet and back through cold Wisconsin winters. Several wrote of pranks they had pulled on Halloween and, after several months of writing, they began to write with humor of ongoing nursing home life. The continuing saga of one woman's adventures with her best friend, her wheelchair, was an eagerly awaited part of the fun at weekly writing classes. It should not be difficult for the teacher to see the possibilities of such humor nor should it be unheard of for the teacher to shed a tear.

* * *

THE SUCCESSFUL TEACHER IS READY FOR:

Laughter and tears
Cancelled and rearranged classes
New friendships
Modest pay
Short times with students and long times alone
The bittersweet knowledge that time is short.

* * *

The peculiar success of those who are writers of poetry does not preclude the possibility that creative writers in other fields can be equally successful. It does indicate that accidental successes arise from the peculiarities of funding patterns and regulations. (Only poets could be hired under a grant from the state arts board.) But insisting on poets emphasizes the need for a writing teacher who is able to hear and see that which has not previously existed, and who values that which exists, presented in new ways and in new combinations. The poet is such a person, but he must also be outwardly turned when with the class; if he is reclusive, he is unsuitable for teaching.

After writers have discovered the joy of writing for their group, they begin to need a wider audience. The teacher's own marketing experience is invaluable. His knowledge of community resources will unlock doors of opportunity for the student that will continue long after the classes end. Seeing his students' work in print, hearing of public readings and performances by students, and meeting them as colleagues in writers' organizations is the ultimate reward for the writer who is also a teacher.

In summary, the ideal teacher is a well-educated, practicing writer who wants to enrich his own life by being a teacher with older adults. He is friendly, well-organized, and respectful of the time of others. He is energetic and not afraid of responsibility, and has the free-lancer's ability to structure his own time and work in various environments comfortably. His students probably will not come to him; he will go to them.

CAN TEACHERS BE NON-WRITERS?

One of the purposes of writing this book is to make the job of teaching easier. The authors have tried to include those things which would have helped them when they began their teaching, and also to include those special insights and resources that were available to them as writers. There seems to be no reason why *enthusiastic readers* cannot be good teachers if they are interested in understanding writing.

The emphasis on writing as a process and writers who see life in a particular way is deliberate. Older people want to like the person working with them, but they also are offended by simple sweetness or cheerful therapeutics when they want to get down to work and keep their minds functioning. They must be treated with respect as writers if the class is to enjoy the success this book promises.

If the teacher who is not a writer does a reasonable amount of research about writing groups and activities in the community, knows the libraries well, and loves reading, this teaching should be fun.

But a warning is in order. Such a person is in serious danger of becoming a writer!

WRITING AS THERAPY

The teacher becomes the colleague of various therapists involved with members of the class. This is especially true in a nursing home or day care center where staff workers will recruit members and bring them to the class. Often people who have suffered brain damage from illness or strokes find that writing helps them to remember. This is an obvious therapeutic aspect of class activity. Less obvious, but just as valued by therapists, are the social and emotional benefits derived from self-expression and *being heard.* Indeed therapists have reported understanding their clients anew through their classroom writing.

* * *

How to Be Over Sixty and Happy Sometimes

I turned me to another thing, and I saw that under the sun, the race is not to the swift, nor the battle to the strong, nor bread to the wise, nor riches to the learned, nor favor to the skillful, but time and chance in all.

I learned that early on in my life and always thought I understood it—until late adulthood.

So I grew up to be a fairly smart kid—an actor, a nurse, a wife, a mother, a grandmother. What's this nagging in my mind? What in hell do I want? Crafts? Learn, do, put away. Not my creation. Travel? I have trouble with motels and require drugs to board a plane or get into a car traveling any distance. Acting? Rejection to be avoided at any cost.

Then one winter's day, I read a newspaper article: "Creative Arts Over Sixty" is offering a course in writing. Well, old girl, writing has to be your own creation, but, dammit, I hate "let's get together because we're over sixty groups." What does that mean? You are some oddity because you can still walk and talk and understand?

I sent my money and I joined that class, and I met a teacher filled with her own credibility as a writer, a gentle, encourag-

ing guide to all the people in her class. The class members were witty, creative, loving people coping gracefully with the transitions in their lives. And the hours were not long enough to listen to the sweet critiques or wait in wonder for the reminiscences, the poetry, and the prose of my classmates.

So I bid you a fond farewell—and remind you that it really is time and chance in all.

—Jo Lynaugh,
for the last day of a writing class
at the Public Library, Madison, Wisconsin

* * *

Chapter 3

Getting Started:
The Beginning Steps
for Starting a Writing Class

*Be there! See it! Hallucinate! Hear it! Feel it! . . . Close your
eyes and don't let yourself write down any words until you can
actually see and hear and touch what you are writing about.*

— *"Writing with Power,"* Peter Elbow

UNDERSTAND YOURSELF AS A WRITER

As an artist coming to teaching, you will need to excavate your
own powers, probe your own accumulated assumptions about art,
and bring to your students whatever riches you can find. Unlike
much subject-oriented teaching, creative writing demands the sharing of essential personal forces as well as ideas. Ideas are necessary,
of course, but they aren't enough. Just as the intellect is only part of
the writing process, so is it merely a partial resource in teaching
writing.

Begin by retracing your own developmental process as an artist.
What led you to where you are now in your work with words? An
autobiographical review will aid you in selecting resources and experiences to bring to new writers. Your own background, after all,
is the story of a successful education. People have come to believe
you are a writer. When did that happen? What has occurred along
the way? What insights have you gained and how did you gain them?
Understanding your own artistic history will be prerequisite to helping others. Outline in writing the milestones of your development,

Retired teacher Florence King enjoys a good laugh in writing class where she often writes for children. Photo by Karen Updike.

listing all the influences you can think of helping yourself to believe you are a worthy prospect for teaching. It will provide you with a private credential. Later you will need to update it because the class experience will add to your ongoing education. But to start out, get a handle on your current artist self. Know who and what you will be taking into the "classroom."

Clarifying your own artistic progress will fortify you somewhat for teaching, but chances are you will continue to feel some uncertainty. Even though you have a writer identity and you are sure you can write—most of the time, anyhow—perhaps you're not so sure you can help others do it. Or maybe you have taught children—novices not only at writing but at life itself. For younger students you at least had the advantage of age and accumulated life experiences. The individuals you will now face are not novices at life. And, unless you are within their age range, they know many things you may not yet have learned yourself. How will you teach such seasoned pupils?

STRUCTURE THE ENVIRONMENT

Sort out your concerns in advance. To begin with, you will need to structure the physical environment. You will want to achieve an atmosphere of comfort and security for the participants, fostering group support when it is needed. You will have to assess the writing background, interests, and needs of each individual. You will need to experiment with ways and means of getting the students to write something, and eventually shape that writing into its best form. You will need to share what you know and believe about writing: what to read, how to use the library, how to discover themes and subjects, and how to evaluate written words. All this may seem formidable if you have not yet met the persons with whom you'll be working. Begin by trusting yourself. Count on your own sensitivity and flexibility to see you through.

Older students will meet you more than half way. They have already been through a life span of learning—all kinds of learning; still they want more. They want to share, talk, laugh, listen, and find out what you know. They want to find out what the other participants know. They are inquiring people who want to keep their minds active. Yet the motivation of seekers will not be all they bring to you; they will bring the reflective judgment of philosophers. Having lived a long time, they are people with ideas and opinions. When they do write, they are likely to have something to say.

Before the class convenes, take a good look at the meeting room. See it as a place where twelve* people, some of whom may come with minor physical liabilities, can sit reasonably comfortably and communicate with each other easily. Each will need a well-lighted work space at a common table. Unless a single table is unusually large, two or more should be clustered into a block. Find out about the room temperature and whether or not you will be able to control it. Be sure there are rest room facilities near the room. Plan your class time segment to best advantage. Assuming a two-hour period, schedule a break at the end of the first hour. Several students will want to stretch and walk around a bit. Try to have coffee and tea available for this time. Informality and physical well-being will promote the mental stimulation you hope to achieve. Eight two-hour meetings will provide an adequate grouping of exposures for one session. Students who want further experience—and many will—should be free to register for subsequent sessions. Some, in fact, will register routinely, session after session, viewing the classes as ongoing support for their evolving identities as writers.

The participants themselves can be expected to provide the writing materials—paper, writing tool, notebook or pocket folder. You might wish to standardize somewhat by requiring a uniform size paper and a preferred implement (typewriter, if available, for home assignments). The reader benefits, of course, when work being offered for critique is double-spaced with adequate margins and prepared on a single side of the paper. Students should be told to retain copies of their work in the event of loss.

INTRODUCTIONS

The day comes. You pack up your artist self and go off to meet the class. Not just any class; a class of adults who have lived six decades or more and know a lot about the world. You know a lot too and now you'll be able to share an exciting realm—writing. This will be an adventure for everyone. Once assembled, introductions will be in order. In many classes held at traditional education institu-

---

*Twelve should be the maximum. This will allow each participant to share a manuscript for critiquing at each meeting.

tions there are no introductions at all, but rather a plunge into the subject at hand by the teacher/authority who uses lecturing to impart his advanced knowledge. If this is not for you—and it should not be in a class of developing writers—you might want to begin with a self-description and encourage the others to follow suit.

* * *

The beginning and the end of all literary activity is the repro-duction of the world that surrounds me by means of the world that is in me, all things being grasped, related, recreated, moulded and reconstructed in a personal form and an original manner.

—Alfred Kazin

* * *

There are other ways to initiate introductions. How about asking for information in written form? This would introduce the writing process immediately, as well as the people. Students might jot down a few words or sentences in response to an assigned subject or question. For example, ask them to complete the following: "When I was young I wanted . . ." and "Now that I am older I want . . ." This avoids the common tendency in verbal introductions to characterize oneself by means of societal roles, e.g., wife, mother, retired farmer, and it provides information of a more intimate nature which interests writers. These brief writings should be shared with the group and supplemented with verbal additions if desired. Encourage further sharing of personal information by asking what more the group would like to know about each individual, based on the writing. Another technique for introductions employs a mini-interview. Students pair off and interview each other two minutes (four minutes total), then each uses the information obtained to introduce his partner to the group. Stress the importance of choosing one or two good questions. Since interviewing is often basic to writing, yet another skill is put to use at the outset. Hopefully, these ideas will spark others and you will find, through experimentation, what works best for you. Experimenting as a teacher is nearly as pleasurable as experimenting with the writing process itself. You will find your students wonderfully cooperative in trying out your ideas.

Gordon Hampel regales fellow writer, Flora Christopher, with his fanciful account of a vagrant vacuum cleaner. Photo by Karen Updike.

FIRST WRITING: THE SENSES

Once you are past introductions, the course is underway. Whatever else you hope to accomplish, give primacy to the actual practice of writing. Students should write in class frequently and outside class every week. They should expect to spend more time on out-of-class writing than they do in class. If you can get them to write daily, all the better. Start out with an in-class exercise the very first day.

The first exercise should be simple yet stimulating, and it should assure a success for all. A sensory stimulus is especially good for introducing new group members to writing. The sense of smell, in particular, is an evocative starting point since it is one of the earliest ways people experience their environment. As infants we smell numerous things and those odors incite feelings of various kinds. And we continue to use this sense and react over a lifetime. Providing an odoriferous substance or object for the writing group establishes a starting point to which nearly every person can relate. You might pass around an assortment of stimulae—cinnamon, mint, vanilla, soap, menthol, coffee, perfume, and shoe polish. Or a single stimulus might go to each individual, all participants receiving the same one perhaps. Following this exposure, give the students a time limit (eight minutes is a good one) and ask them to write of what the odor reminded them.

Any form is acceptable for this effort—single words, lists, phrases, paragraphs, poems, stories, jokes, fantasies or reminiscences. When the allotted time is up, have them share the results. The variety that occurs will be a source of delight in individual differences. In commenting on their readings, point out specific achievements—a well-chosen adjective, good sensory language, an original comparison, an interesting anecdote. In this way you will be practicing the art of encouragement while giving attention to some of the elements of good writing.

RESPONSE TO THE WRITING

The overall tone for all responses to spontaneous exercises must be positive and enthusiastic. A hastily prepared manuscript done in the presence of the group will certainly have flaws, but the group need not dwell on them. Rather it should acclaim any response—a polished one on the first day being somewhat an overachievement. Some students take these "beginnings" and develop them outside of class into fuller, more finished forms. Encourage this. The initial goal, however, will simply be to stimulate some kind of writing by everyone, to celebrate its accomplishment, and to enjoy the various results.

* * *

Why, after seventy, did I start to write stories . . . an attempt to put pieces of myself together? We talk as if the problem of identity were a problem of youth, but the question of who we are is always with us and if anything gets worse. The world seems always to be breaking us into pieces, and we keep always yearning, if I may use a theological phrase, for some sort of unity of the soul.

—*Norman Maclean*

Items evoking other sense responses are good follow-ups for sub-sequent meetings: colors, sounds, textures, and tastes. Just as our senses lead us from birth onward into all human experiencing and sharing, so do they take us into the writer's realm where we do it all again—selectively—with words. The beginning writer must see, hear, smell, touch, and taste anew with an added purpose. He must become a person on whom nothing is lost. To this end, you will need to arrange encounters which will lead the student to experience varied events—some drawn from memory, some from the unconscious (dreams), some oriented in the here and now—and urge the distillation and transformation of these encounters into words, words which are fresh, original and interesting, words which become poems, stories, essays or plays.

OTHER WRITING STIMULAE

There are other options for in-class exercises and home assignments. In lieu of a tangible sensory object, common experiences or emotions are possibilities. For example, students might write about their breakfast that morning, the trip from home to the center they are now in, a celebration they once participated in, or a loss they have had to work through. These assignments will prove to be especially valuable to individuals who are slow to develop their own writing ideas. They might be used as a routine warm-up exercise for each class meeting. All groups find them fun to come back to occasionally, even when ideas are plentiful. Sensitivity to participants' needs, of course, will be an essential guideline for you in selecting and scheduling any activities.

GROUP PROCESS

The group is a powerful means for promoting the study and practice of writing. For the elderly person, joining an assemblage of others in similar circumstances—all of whom share a mature sense of time over a life span of varied and lengthy relationships and an accumulation of common historical events—is stimulating and satisfying. Other elders as fellow group members are appealing, not only for social exchange, but also because they are the best help in assuaging the individual's initial fear that writing may not be among his talents and capabilities or that he is coming to it too late. Any beginning writer needs the reactions of others if he is to gain perspective and confidence. Other writers can understand the realities of his experience and applaud his efforts. Other writers can serve as critics, motivate theme and technique ideas, suggest resources and market possibilities, and offer their own work as models. The group's essential role is to stimulate and encourage the individual. As teacher, you will want to affirm that support function at the outset. Older students learn it quickly and practice it consistently.

* * *

I've come to learn for myself how little one needs, in the art of writing, to convey the lot, and how a lot of words, on the other hand, can convey so little.

— *"Loitering With Intent," Muriel Spark*

* * *

MODELS AND RESOURCES

Each class, including the first, presents the opportunity to expose the group to the work of skillful, accomplished writers—local or widely known. Choices for the first day might include a poem, a short story, an essay or a passage from a novel. Selection might be determined by a timely news event, the season, the already-mentioned topic of senses, aging, or the writing process itself. Based on the current assumption that students are curious about the teacher's creations, you may share some of your own work at this time. The works chosen will necessarily be short and have appeal for the individuals expected to attend the first class. They should lead to the appreciation of effective writing without overwhelming or puzzling the listener. When photocopying is possible, some of these selections might be copied and distributed for more careful study outside of class. The reading of widely published writers not only provides a pleasurable experience for the group; it also offers the opportunity to discuss the reasons for the works' impact and the techniques employed. E. B. White, Robert Frost, Emily Dickinson, and many other familiar authors can be counted on to enchant, yet provide material for analysis as well. And published writers in the local region—especially older ones—are frequently a gift of discovery. They seem to offer a more attainable model and, if living, are possibly accessible for the students to hear at readings or other writers' gatherings.

Suggesting writers' resources for students to explore outside the classroom is another function of the class. Magazines, journals, guides, reference books, the public library, contests, conferences, workshops, other classes, and organizations related to writing are all relevant to the group's ongoing learning. You will be in the best position to determine the proper timing of resource introduction, which cannot be all at once. Some resources may be appropriate for mention the first day, however—especially upcoming community events such as poetry readings or the basics of library usage for the completion of a home assignment. Strunk and White's *Elements of Style* and Babette Deutsch's *A Poetry Handbook* are good books to recommend early in the course, as are the magazines *Writer's Digest* and *The Writer.*

ASSIGNMENTS

A final major consideration in getting a new group started is the assignment of work to be completed outside the classroom. In-class exercises are beneficial as originators of ideas and demonstrations that many kinds of stimulae can prompt the writer to produce a short first draft. More refined, finished work usually requires time and solitude. It may require research. During the week between classes the student has time to develop more properly a work in whatever form is suggested or chosen.

In assigning homework, take into account the needs, interests and backgrounds of students. An individual who does not understand paragraph structuring may find the assignment to write an essay disturbing; yet he may produce a very good limerick. Conversely, some essay writers may never produce a limerick. Thematic assignments bearing open-ended form possibilities may be the answer to this dilemma. Form restrictions which intimidate the beginning writer are thus avoided. For the thematic assignment, all students receive a common topic to work with, but the final form may vary according to individual preference. Thus the assignment to write about an early childhood memory may lead to a narrative poem, an adult short story, a biographical prose account, and a children's story within the same group. This provides variety in the manuscripts and the students are able to learn from each other's assorted pursuits. Later on, following some successes, students who are reluctant to experiment with forms not previously tried may benefit from an occasional assignment based on a specific form. Both types of assignment will probably have their respective places sometime during the course. In starting out, however, the thematic approach allows students the comfort of what seems easiest and provides the teacher with evidence of their needs and interests. Topics especially effective for early home assignments include: a place where you can relax and be your real self; a gift you gave someone; your earliest childhood memory; a special friend; or an object you own which has special meaning for you.

In an eight-week course, the seven home assignments should offer a range of experiences. Some will probably be based on form considerations; they will also be designed to stimulate new ways of thinking, both about the world and about writing. For the new writer there should be an ongoing dual process of discovery—inner and outer, as he probes his own creative responses and receives the impact of other work. As previously mentioned, these assignments might expose the student to the library; or they might train his ear for dialogue, encourage him to experiment with make-believe, expose him to published writers and critics. Perhaps they will bring him to intimacy with his own dreams and his own memory. In all cases, making the homework optional, yet emphasizing the advantages of completing it, is the best strategy. This places with the student the responsibility for learning what homework has to teach. The older student will understand the principle involved: you get out of something what you put into it.

* * *

What makes good poetry for me a is a terrible specificity of detail, whether of object or of feeling. The poet names and particularizes and thus holds for a moment in time (and thus for all time, as long as time lasts for humanity) whatever elusive event he/she is drawn to. By terrible, I mean unflinching. Honest and sometimes compassionate.

—Maxine Kumin

THE WORKSHOP

Participation in a writing class should be in part synonymous with participation in a writing workshop. For the individual this means preparing manuscripts to submit for group evaluation and revising them following group responses plus active listening and thoughtful reaction to the work of others. Since the latter function gets practiced immediately, it needs clarification at the outset of the workshop. Often one must *learn* to be an insightful, helpful critic. That skill may not come naturally. A common problem with older adults is the tendency to offer praise with little discrimination. The elderly population in creative arts classes seems to be especially accepting and tolerant of its own. All too often the sole initial response to a written work is, "Oh, that's good!" Even when the piece is indeed good, the critic must learn to identify the specific elements that make it so, and to offer an expanded statement. On the other hand, in spite of the preponderance of praise, there are individuals who find an occasional fault and are so pleased with their detective skills that they zero in on it relentlessly. Here perspective must be maintained and the overall quality of the work appreciated in spite of the revealed flaw.

As suggested previously, you as teacher will serve as a model for critiquing and will elaborate on the elements of good writing as they come up in the review of manuscripts. You will provide guidelines for critiquing which emphasize accomplishments rather than shortcomings. A good resource for this is Peter Elbow's *Writing With Power.* Yet you will not hesitate to suggest revisions or experimental changes which might bring improvement. If a manuscript is already good, but can be further strengthened, push for that final polish even though the writer feels satisfied with what he has done. The possibility of excellence need not be precluded because the student appears to be a fragile, elderly person who will never publish, or for whom reworking seems to be too much trouble. Every writer risks as he writes, and that risk deserves quality attention which is serious and honest.

Chapter 4

Continuing With Writing: Keeping Up Interest and Participation

If at first students seem to relish being students again, taking a real class from a real teacher just as in the nostalgic school days of their youth, you can be sure they will tire of the novelty if they have not discovered in their early writing class something special and unique, something different from the gratifications of a well-played bridge hand or a well-run bazaar. What really hooks them on writing is their new-found sense that they still have the capacity to explore and discover things about themselves and their world, past and present.

After five years of offering writing classes at senior centers, we have had to take stock of some curious developments. Older adults though they are, they insist on improving! They tell their experiences with more technique, they select better details, they edit themselves more effectively, they risk writing about more sensitive subjects. The classes are not therefore simply pastimes. They insist on enrolling again and again, sometimes even in advance, to ensure a place and the continuance of the program. The leadership or teacher aspect of having a writing group was evidently important. Centers with strong writing programs, thought to no longer need a teacher, ceased to meet regularly when no teacher was provided. Sociability, even a regular forum in which to be heard, was evidently not sufficient impetus to keep them writing and to keep them coming.

* * *

The craft of writing is personal, but all writers share the common task of having to turn out many words, as a gymnast expects to do thousands of turns before getting one right.

—Ruth Kanin

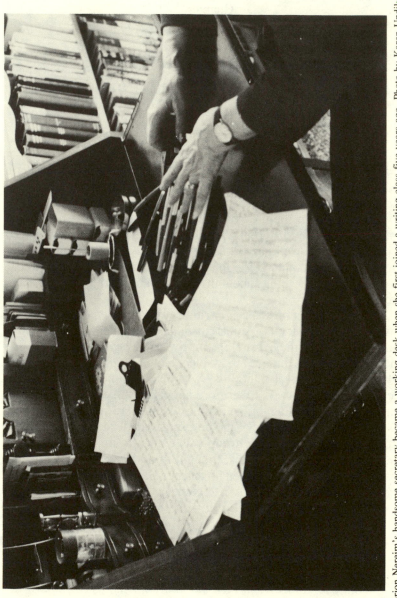

Marion Nereim's handsome secretary became a working desk when she first joined a writing class five years ago. Photo by Karen Updike.

We began to wonder whether the way we treated them and their manuscripts might not be key factors. The point was not so much to be heard, but to be listened to in a certain way; not so much to be read and enjoyed briefly, superficially, but to have their work taken seriously enough to be thought about and criticized with an eye to making it even more effective. That must be what was making writing class so satisfying. Spending time with each other was not enough; attending to each other with great effort and concentration produced quite a different story.

Good teaching is usually meant to lead the student out into independence from the teacher. Not so with the teaching of older adults. When one of us described what we did in a class, a stranger replied, "You're not a teacher, you're a coach!" The need for on-going stimulation and motivation of older adults makes the teacher's presence a must. This holds true for short and long term projects. Older adults are sometimes inclined to withdraw, to diminish or curtail the number and type of projects to which they will make a commitment. Our job as teachers is to get them positively addicted, get them hooked on being heard, get them hungering after the wonderful "writer's high" that comes after the completion of a piece of work.

The first series of writing classes can focus on the importance of using images, and priming the pump to show them how much they do in fact have to write about. In later classes, students can explore forms other than the one they use most frequently, discover the value of taking teacher-written editorial suggestions and in-class comments to heart in revising a manuscript, and acquaint themselves with the useful techniques of keeping a writer's journal and marketing file for their work.

* * *

In old age, things become more intense rather than less so. Things get more poignant—so many associations—everything reverberating with everything else.

—John Hall Wheelock

* * *

It is usually more effective to suggest ideas to write about than literary forms to imitate. The writing ideas may be drawn from subjects great writers have handled remarkably well, as Kenneth Koch illustrates in his book *Rose, Where Did You Get That Red?* Or they may be inspired by psychology, the graphic arts, music or dramatic productions. Because of the obvious intimidation that occurs from feeling one has to compete with William Blake or Robert Frost, we do not recommend reading a published or "great" poem upon a subject until the group has tried its hand at it. It is better to digest the idea of a poem yourself and then suggest that the class write a piece in which they tell about the same thing from their own experience. You might suggest that every sentence ask a question of some object in nature. Or suggest they talk in a perfectly natural voice to some powerful force in nature that awes them. Only after they have done this should you produce copies of "Tiger Tiger Burning Bright" or "Ode to the West Wind." Because some of our classes were held with rural populations, we used Robert Frost's poem, "You Come Too," to drive home the idea that there are unique things to be seen even in the commonplace farm chores of cleaning out the pasture spring or bringing in a newborn calf from the fields. The successive writing idea was to invite someone to go along with them to do some fairly routine activity that nevertheless possesses something wonderful about it. After they are more confident and quite familiar with this method of offering them a writing idea, it matters less if a "real" poem is read first to them. They see it simply as one author's treatment of the idea. It is of course less intimidating if the author is not well known and famous, but just another interested, aware person, reacting to his world. Older adults just becoming acquainted with the idea that art is made by regular people out of their own life experiences are still struggling with reservations about suitability of subjects and their own particular competence. One published poet ruefully recalls a reading after which he was asked, "Were those real poems you read or were they something you just wrote down?"

* * *

Writers may not be special—sensitive or talented in any usual sense. They are simply engaged in sustained use of a language skill we all have. Their 'creations' come about through confident reliance on stray impulses that will, with trust, find occasional patterns that are satisfying.

—William Stafford

Maybelle Riach is serious about her humor. She delights readers with her honest and funny accounts of every day life. Photo courtesy of The Wisconsin State Journal.

Virtually any poem or story that genuinely intrigues you as a reader will contain the germ of a writing idea for class which you will be able to sell with enthusiasm. A poem about regret in The New Yorker could prompt you to ask them to list ten things they regret, then choose three of the most poignant to tell more about. Another poem suggested to us that they could write about how many different people they think they have been in their life. Another, to tell about a time when they felt totally caught up in some sort of imaginative play within their family circle, and what effect such playing had had. Examples of writing ideas generated by poems could go on and on. Kenneth Koch has a fine suggestion of eventually asking students to list all of the things they have written about as a sort of 'list' poem in the vein of Robert Herrick's poem, "Delight in Disorder." Marion Nereim's poem, "I Sing" is a good example of the result.

I Sing

I sing of Spring
  Of exultation rising up within me.
I sing of my Helpmate
  Of our years together.
I sing of my Children
  Of their courage and competence.
I sing of my Grandchildren
  My immortality.
I sing of my Brothers and Sisters
  Each overcoming his Gethsemane.
I sing of my Ancestors
  Forever pioneers.
I sing of the core of Strength
  Within us all.

—Marion Nereim

Should you become interested in a specific theme yourself, such as death, growth, denial, or physical fitness, you can organize three or four writing assignments around this theme, illustrating it with works drawn from different literary forms. When you read the literature upon which the writing idea was based each week, you will be able to operationally define various rhetorical devices, what is meant by point of view, voice, stanzaic form, and so forth. Until the group is experienced it is not advisable to prescribe the particular form an experience must take. Even if you have focused four or five classes on elements of the short story, it is not wise to insist that they respond to the writing idea with a short story. It is more important that they write each time than that they comply with the assignment.

* * *

Poetry is the heartbeat of life. Poems are life transmuted into diamonds, compact and indestructible. The first literature of every country is its poetry. It is the oldest language we have, the most primitive, the most elemental, the most natural expression of ourselves as human beings.

—Unknown

* * *

In the beginning it is effective to suggest writing ideas designed to free students from the tyranny of being too outer-directed and adaptable at the expense of their real selves. You might suggest periodically that they "Tell about something you know very well, but put a lie in every sentence," or "tell about something you dared not tell anybody when you were a child" or "brag unabashedly about something of which you are genuinely very proud." Many of these ideas are to be found in Koch's books.

Since good stories, poems, and plays always show new growth, new understandings attained, it is wise to focus writing ideas that will help older adults face times of loss, suffering, and change in their past and present lives. Koch suggests making a poem by starting every sentence "I used to" and finishing it, "but now I." This exercise illustrates to them that they are in fact changing. Other writing ideas might include the following: Ask them to describe the place they felt safest as a child, to describe the place where they learned something very important about what life is all about, to tell about the time one of their parents died, about a time they thought they could do anything, when they were pre-schoolers, when they were teenagers. Ask them to tell about something they love well because they know they must leave it before long. Ask them to reconstruct their childhood explanation of why bad things happen and contrast it with how that explanation has changed. Suggest they tell about a time they were glad they had lied, or about a time they tried to kid themselves. Groups of poems or stories resulting from this kind of thematic approach to writing assignments make strong personal statements.

* * *

What really shapes and conditions and makes us . . . is somebody only a few of us ever have the courage to face; and that is the child you once were, long before formal education ever got its claws into you—that impatient, all-demanding child who wants love and power and can't get enough of either and who goes on raging and weeping in your spirit 'til at last your eyes are closed and all the fools say, "Doesn't he look peaceful?" It is those pent up, craving children who make all the wars and all the horrors and all the art and all the beauty and discovery in life, because they are trying to achieve what lay beyond their grasp before they were five years old.

—"The Rebel Angels," Robertson Davies

* * *

It is wise to acquaint continuing students with the value of journal keeping. Urge them to spend a minimum of ten minutes a day jotting down ideas, observations, sense impressions that crossed their consciousness that day. Suggest they clip or copy phrases or paragraphs they discover in their reading to which they particularly respond. Suggest that they preserve fleeting ideas for stories, ballads, occasional poems, articles, interviews in their journals until they can tackle them. Explain that it is fun to review your journal; it is almost like reading a book about yourself. If they do review their journal every other week or so, they will be able to chart their imaginative course and be in a better position to begin giving themselves assignments. Story ideas generated by class reading of other people's work should also be recorded there for future use. Should they have nothing to record that day, they can use the minimum amount of time at least describing any object in the room or seen from the window in a "free-writing" fashion, that is, writing without stopping for a specific period of time, proceeding in a chain of association, stream-of-consciousness manner. Subjects from earlier assignments could also be used for this journal exercise.

A writer is a gunner, sometimes waiting in his blind for something to come in, sometimes roaming the countryside hoping to scare something up. Like other gunners, he must cultivate patience; he may have to work many covers to bring down one partridge.

—William Strunk Jr. and E. B. White

* * *

Be sensitive to how much editing a student can tolerate without becoming discouraged. Some writers have no intention of reworking a draft and do not like to see all the things they could conceivably improve. It disheartens them. Others request and take to heart the corrections you can provide. Handing out a sheet of symbols of editor's short-hand corrections facilitates making suggestions on their work. If there are many things that could be corrected, choose two major ones and let the others slide for the time being. Whether the manuscript is heavily edited or not, it is always a good idea to return the papers with some personal comment or reaction to the work as a whole. You might direct them to certain authors or other older writers with whom they might like to share papers. You might offer marketing suggestions or suggest an article or longer project based on this subject. Whatever the case, do not miss the opportunity to write personal notes. You may type them on a small sheet of paper and clip it to the manuscript, or ask the writer to leave space on his manuscript for your comments by starting half way down the first page.

In reading their poetry it is especially important not to improve and change a word or line arbitrarily. It is better to write a question or suggestion, and let them come up with their own improvement. In all editing, it is advisable to let the spirit of their work and discovery override your idea of how it ought to be done.

* * *

The purpose of art is beauty—one of the antique and perennial pleasures of our species which weds us to the world and makes us love it . . . feelings normally so truant and ephemeral as to be uncapturable, in poetry are richly set down and formed into an avenue of unfamiliar truth.

—Frederick Turner

Hazel Briggs Rice searches for just the right word for one of her popular short stories. Photo courtesy of The Wisconsin State Journal.

Chapter 5

Acceptance and Beyond:
Rewards for Writers

Old Uncle

We called him Mr. Stuart,
most called him "Uncle."
Folks said he was a Quaker.
He and his sister's husband,
who was our Civil War veteran,
carried the mail from
the post-office to the train
and from the train to the post-office.

He always wore a baggy suit coat
that never matched his trousers,
with an old felt hat
upon his shock of snowy hair.

Bright blue eyes,
rheumy and red-rimmed,
could barely see the world
that lay beyond
a bulbous nose and graying beard.

I was eleven then,
always hung around the depot
near train time.
A gopher lived across the tracks,
in a hole right next to the coal bin.

One day it was eating corn
spilled upon the ground,
and I up and threw a rock.

Hit it, killed it dead!
Bragging, held it up for all to see.

Old Uncle's half seeing,
red-rimmed eyes looked out at me,
"Poor wee beastie," he softly said,
"he did no harm to thee."

—Benjamin Brothers

When the intense self-reflection of the elderly generates writing to share with others, older people in writing groups coalesce with profound feelings of belonging. Add to this cohesiveness and increased pride in accomplishment a greater feeling of being understood and renewed involvement in society in general, and the reasons for writing groups for the elderly seem obvious.

It is, of course, not that simple, but five years of experience with such groups have shown us that older people will participate in writing groups and that they do benefit far beyond anything we had initially expected. While discussion groups are beneficial, the more exacting demands of writing help the individual to focus clearly, an asset which carries over into talking as well. Through writing we have seen people begin to regain memory lost through strokes and gradually find their own ways back to remembering. Some people cannot remember words they want to say, although they find that they can write them.

The author of the poem at the beginning of this chapter had simply never had time to write. He had been too busy with the demands of rearing a family on a farm. Some longing brought him to a writing group. The teacher recognized the gift of poetry and encouraged it. As the group gradually came to expect poetry from him, his confidence increased. He is now a member of his state fellowship of poets and an active writer. Others come to class with long writing histories but believe their writing days are over. Appreciative listeners and assignments that encourage new ways of self-expression change their minds.

Belonging to a writing group provides stimulation not only to write but to read and stretch to see another's point of view. Sensory exercises help members become more aware of things around them: wild flowers among cinders on a driveway, the view from a window, the talk in a shopping mall, the smell of cinnamon or shoe polish. Gradually this awareness frees people to talk about heretofore forbidden subjects such as feelings about being old, opinions about our laws, resentments about the lack of generosity shown toward and by the old.

IT'S ALL RIGHT TO WRITE

The teacher seems somehow to give permission to write, to think of oneself as a writer. Amidst life's superficialities, the journey toward intimacy one undertakes in a writing group can be enormously exciting. The reassurance that this excitement, this new commitment, is all right comes first from the teacher and then from the group.

Beginning to see one's life as the stuff of literature is for many a sharp contradiction to earlier experiences with literature as remote or boring. As the individual develops his own voice and finds that people like it, his writing style evolves. When others value his experiences as universal he feels less lonely and more ready to share himself. Each person says things in his own unique way, and as others come to value this uniqueness, all know joy and delight in their differences and in their discoveries of each other. This discovery is acceptance and beyond.

* * *

A poem is a part of me dressed in words for you to see.

—Benjamin Brothers

* * *

WRITING AND THE FAMILY

As individuals develop more clarity in self-expression, they build a bridge to other family members. When their families read what they have written, the writers feel they have been heard. Family members come to see the older person not only with love but with respect for what he *is* doing. One woman who worked doggedly revising, improving, deleting trite and cute statements, condensing, and highlighting dramatic details finally won a major prize in a state contest. Her children told her with joy, ''Mother, your writing is getting so much better!'' She knew this was true. They were respecting her for what she was actually doing. Outside recognition may also help to prevent older people from relying too much on only their families for emotional support.

WRITING AS COMPENSATION

One woman who has lived in a nursing home for many years told us that writing is what she lives for; we saw her become a gregarious leader in the writing group. She later won a prize for an essay about her father and has had many pieces published in the local newspaper and in the nursing home newsletter. She is a person of meticulous good taste who knows her writing is improving. She could not be deceived or flattered and would be grossly offended by empty compliments.

The value of developing writing skills when speech is no longer possible is difficult to calculate. A man who has been paralyzed for seven years, unable even to speak, wrote to President Reagan about his gratitude to his therapists and his newfound excitement in the writing group. As a member of a writing group he rocked with silent laughter as others read what they had written, and thoroughly enjoyed having others appreciate his efforts. His grandchildren in a distant city receive copies of what he writes and he has been published in the local newspaper.

Many older people have spent their lives doing service-oriented activities but have not done anything for just themselves. Paradoxically, as they write for their own pleasure, they often reach others as they have not previously been able to do. It becomes acceptable for them to take themselves seriously. A man who had not written poetry until well into his sixties is amazed that other people of all ages are moved by what he writes. His poems have won prizes but they have also brought him friendship.

FEELING GOOD ABOUT YOURSELF

All of this, of course, enhances self-esteem. We hear them say, ''I write things people enjoy,'' ''I had the guts to join a writing group,'' and ''I still can learn.'' This feeling of worth is reinforced by tangible rewards. Having writing published is enormously satis-

Writer Grace Bracker and co-editor Lenore M. Coberly look over proofs for Heartland Journal, a magazine especially for writers over sixty years of age. Photo courtesy of the Milwaukee Journal, Brent Nicastro photographer.

fying and sometimes financially rewarding as well. There are many contests and the whole group is likely to celebrate when one member wins a prize. Presenting programs based on writing for community groups is fun but most important is the fact that each time a writer takes part in a writing exercise or writes outside of class he has a product which others can appreciate and which is a source of pride. A writer must be continually growing and becoming more effective if he is to be satisfied at any age.

When illness strikes, members of the writing groups are ideally equipped to keep in touch with the absent member. When a member returns discouraged by lost abilities, the other members are quick to appreciate what can be done and to encourage trying.

GETTING FAMILY HISTORY INTO WRITING

Writing family history is a non-threatening way to come to writing; regular practice will help to focus the writing, thus making it more interesting. Most families ask their older members to write down their memories without understanding that the older person fears that his stories are likely to be repetitive and heard as boring. Sometimes the older person can easily write well-crafted pieces before he comes to the classes and needs only to be told that they are good. A Missouri woman who had long lived in Wisconsin and had taken an active part in community affairs was confined to a nursing home following a stroke. When she found interest among the class members in her stories of Missouri she compiled a book of poetry and stories. It was sold by a bank in her home town in Missouri and required a second printing!

SEEING EACH PERSON'S VALUE

Literature is, after all, life. To be valued for what you write is to be valued as a person. To give this value to another is a great reward also. Members of the writing classes are enthusiastic about one another's work and often come to see each other in new and exciting ways. A gentle southern lady who wrote quietly of riding the street car or choosing hair ribbons came to class one day with an account of an older woman who visited an attractive older man in his home for a week-end but decided against marrying him. She refused to identify it as fiction or non-fiction but her eyes sparkled as they had not done before and she began to join the group who usually went to the drug store for coffee after class.

FEAR OF BEING BORING

The fear of being boring is a great burden to many older people. Specific exercises help to overcome both the reason for this and the tendency to wander from one subject to another. In writing one develops a sense of timing, learns how to hold the punch line, cultivates appreciation for the vivid and concrete while avoiding the general. Simple exercises involving the senses and memory are often all that is needed to put fragmented stories together.

GROWING APPRECIATION FOR THE CRAFT

Practicing the craft of writing helps the writer to enjoy the writing of others. Enthusiasm for literature grows as examples are studied in class. Reading for content and reading for the craft are different and those trying to write soon discover it. Practice in any art deepens appreciation for the work of the artist.

* * *

. . . it is occasionally possible, just for brief moments, to find the words that will unlock the doors of all those many mansions inside the head and express something—perhaps not much, just something—of the crush of information that presses in on us from the way a crow flies over and the way a man walks and the look of a street and from what we did one day a dozen years ago.

—Ted Hughes

* * *

A superb story-teller who had few writing skills came to a writing group. She often stayed up all night writing wonderful stories which the teacher would cover with purple ink, the color for correction.

Gradually her papers had less purple and she began to win prizes for her stories. When a new member joined the group and each older member was asked to tell what the class was about, the nocturnal story-teller told how her papers had formerly been covered with purple and she said, "Now I miss those marks!"

READY TO MOVE ON

Because the need for each individual to know who he is grows with age as does his store of life material, it is easy to see why older people, once convinced they can do it, make good writers. As students become more confident, they go beyond the writing class into classes for all ages, writers' conferences, summer workshops, community programs, and writers' organizations. Afternoons at a marsh or city park take on new meaning and purpose. Magical hours at the library are doubly valued when they yield material for writing and for sharing with writing friends.

We see groups of older writers having coffee together, at used book sales, and at awards banquets. What has age, after all, to do with it, once you begin to write?

* * *

Ah! but verses amount to so little when one writes them young. One ought to wait and gather sense and sweetness a whole life long, and a long life if possible, and then, quite at the end, one might perhaps be able to write ten lines that were good.

—Rainer Maria Rilke

* * *

Chapter 6

Classes in a Nursing Home Setting: Unique Possibilities for Mental Stimulation and Fun in Nursing Homes and Day Centers

Pine

Feel the roughness
Natural for needles to be rough
Needles spring back
Wind blows them, bends them
When the wind stops, the tree springs back up.
Whole limbs spring back when bent.
If the limb is too heavy and is bent too far,
    it breaks.
As long as people are able they can spring back like branches,
    but if they get crippled they can't spring back.
In winter time when a tree gets heavy with ice and snow,
It bends and sometimes breaks.
We saw that one year, during the ice storm a lot of trees
    broke down from the heavy burden.
That depends upon the strength of the tree
Whether or not it will break under stress.
Even you or me, we could lift a lot more
When we were eighteen or twenty years old.
A young tree would stand more than an older tree.

—George Brockmiller

Looking at Candy Corn

I see a bright red Indian tepee
with yellow fall flowers around it.
The white top seems to be smoke,
maybe from a peace pipe.

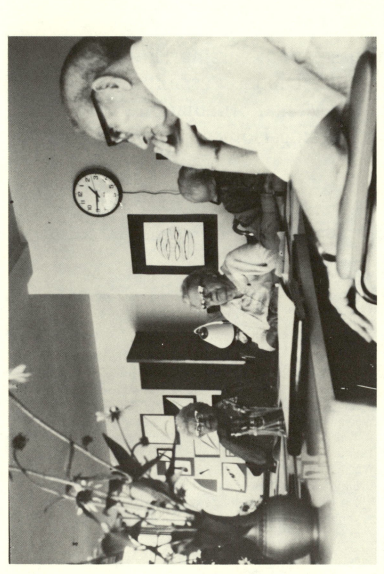

Time passes quickly when friends read in writing class. Isabel Houser, Elsie McKee, George Brockmiller, and Bill Rathbun never missed a class. Photo courtesy of Capital Times.

But I am on a diet.
Anyway I can't eat
an Indian tepee.

—Isabel Houser

Dogs

I can't get over how some dogs
   lead the blind.
I had a dog who used to sit
   on the back of my kiddy-car.
His name was Skipper.

When I came here
I had to give him up.

Terrible to mourn a dog,
   but I do.

—Jeanne Emerson

Sitting By the Window

I see beautiful fall leaves—
yellow, red, and orange.
Leaves gradually drop
from the trees
bright against the green grass.
But I see another picture—
the ground is covered with snow
Brrrrrrrrrrrrrrr
Changing seasons is kinda fun.
It is something
to look forward to.
But I do like warm weather
and so does my arthritis.

—Elsie McKee

I drove slowly that day. I didn't want to get to where I was
going and I knew a lot of reasons why. There was no one in my
acquaintance who had taught creative writing at the county
nursing home. I had found accounts of only two persons in my

reading who had tried and neither had accomplished very much or worked at it for very long. Failure to achieve anything was a very real possibility and frightening revelations of suffering and defeat seemed certain.

These words are from a reminiscence essay by a writing teacher who had gone on to teach successfully in a nursing home for three years. The essay was entitled "Wherein a Teacher's Ignorance is Dispelled," and changed when published in a local paper to "Class Learns Value of Writing." It struck a responsive chord in readers who very much wanted to overcome their own fears of nursing homes.

* * *

They might not need me; but they might.
I'll let my head be just in sight;
A smile as small as mine might be
Precisely their necessity.

—*Emily Dickinson*

* * *

It would be less than honest to deny that there are enormous problems for teachers in this setting compared to those working in senior centers, libraries, and other places convenient to the mobile elderly, but the success and growth achieved by members of the nursing home class were far beyond the expectations of both the teacher and the regular staff. And the teacher did lose her fear of nursing homes, a reward that is hard to value too highly.

Rewards for writers mentioned in Chapter 5 are experienced by nursing home patients but in differing degrees. Being a part of a group where they really communicate with one another is as important to the confined person as to those isolated in their own homes, but becoming a part of the larger writing community is not a reasonable goal. The teacher who sees the patients as writers, takes them seriously, and shows respect for their work will soon begin to enjoy the classes.

The classroom is usually the sunroom at the end of the hall or a crafts room which is shared with the writing class when not in use.

The staff may set up tables but it is important to arrange them so that they make a square rather than a long table. Hearing and seeing problems make getting as close together as possible important. The square also helps the teacher not to become isolated from those far down the table.

Sometimes when the teacher arrives and walks down the hall she feels depression like polluted air that everyone is breathing. When a problem exists in the home, it is likely to be shared by all. One such problem was created when the management of a home decided to stop cooking meals on the premises and to bring pre-cooked food in by truck. The loss of the sounds and smells of cooking was overwhelming to the residents. It was useless to try to write about that day's subject of spring and gardening. They wrote instead about their feelings of loss and the results were taken to the officials responsible for the change. They described what it was like to line up in the hall in wheel chairs and smell food cooking, how satisfying it was to sometimes help the cooks, and how much they liked having jars of peanut butter on the table. The writing was so affecting that a compromise was reached whereby some of the food was prepared at the home. The teacher must be prepared to accept needs outside of her planned program.

At least half of the seating space should be arranged to accommodate wheel chairs, many of which can be placed close to the table so that knees fit under the table. Others may have attached tables or oxygen tanks and other medical devices. These need extra space but should be as close to the table as possible. One patient with multiple sclerosis was brought to class on a portable couch, a device that may be used more in the future.

* * *

No one is useless in this world who lightens the burden of it to anyone else.

—Charles Dickens

* * *

Class members who can walk often push their colleagues down the hall in their wheel chairs. Nurses also help to assemble the class. In spite of the most heroic efforts some patients who can benefit from being a part of a writing group cannot come to the classroom. The teacher may visit these writers in their rooms, pick up their manuscripts, leave assignments, and return manuscripts with the comments of other class members written on them.

It is rare to find typed work in the nursing home but seeing their work in type is exciting and encouraging to the writers. The teacher who types the manuscripts each week will come not only to know their work, but to understand how it was constructed. Being a writer himself, he may see in the typing the way the mind of the author has worked. It is an almost mystical experience which makes the extra work tolerable. In addition to giving importance to the student's work, the typed copy is also useful for display and for sending to relatives. It can, of course, be photocopied when needed.

Colorful folders provided at the first meeting of the class helps members to keep their work together and makes them realize that their work is valued. Paper with wide lines and soft pencils are good for work in class.

The teacher needs to be friendly, sociable, and able to accept the conditions of the patients, not without sympathy, but with simplicity. Beyond this, when he begins to see them as writers, and himself as among writers, they begin to see themselves in that way.

WRITING DONE FROM INTERVIEWS

Perhaps as many as half of the class will be physically unable to write their manuscripts. This has proven to be a problem but not an insurmountable one. The clear and constant emphasis upon writing, not speaking, leads even those who verbalize what they want written to focus and carefully select their material. Patients who have previously talked all of the time, repeating the same story over and over, have responded well to friendly reminders that it is necessary not to say what we want to write or have written, lest it be lost before we are ready to write.

Actual writing must be done in every class session. When an assignment is made the teacher can simply interview those members unable to write while others are writing. Tact is required in identifying these persons since some may simply be illiterate. Take their word when they say they prefer to be interviewed. Three or four interviews can easily be conducted while the class writes, usually for about twenty minutes. If there are more than that to be interviewed you will need a helper. The interview results will tend to be shorter but often have the quality of poetry. The results of the interviews should be read along with the written pieces, going around the table in order, beginning each time with a different writer, whether the patient reads his own or has it read.

* * *

I was gratified to be able to answer promptly and I did. I said I didn't know.

—*Mark Twain*

* * *

Those interviewed will include members with serious problems with sight, palsied or stroke victims, people with degenerative diseases, and those who have lost or injured their hands. In this setting the teacher needs to have developed skill in interviewing, which non-fiction writers usually have. Honest interest in what the student has to say is fundamental, but a fine line between putting words in their mouths and actively encouraging response must be always in the teacher's mind. He must make suggestions to some people sometimes. For example, a man who has worked as a farm laborer all of his life was unable to think of anything to say about childhood play. He had not gone to school, he had not had toys, his family had had no games or books. However, a sympathetic and creative interviewer discovered that he had known every plant and animal in the pine woods near his home. Many stories flowed from that discovery.

An apparently catatonic woman who had refused to raise her head responded to an interviewer's enthusiastic comments about her brightly colored dress and produced a piece about her love of color and flowers. She remained an active member of the class from that time on, listening to others and smiling and showing delight when her piece was read. Others in the group came to enjoy her. One day she asked the teacher to write that she liked her red dress because people talked to her when she wore it. The typed copy of that piece was carefully carried back to her room and put into her desk.

The sounds of talk and laughter in the quiet setting of a nursing home attracts visitors who are likely to remain in the hall listening.

Cane and wheelchair do not prevent George Brockmiller and Marilyn Peterson from participating fully in a writing class. Photo courtesy of Creative Arts Over Sixty.

This attention gives the members of the class a feeling of pride. They very much enjoy having an end-of-semester party during which they read, or have read, something which they have written and refreshments are served. Nearly everyone in the home is likely to attend. A little book of student work is a nice last day gift and provides a copy to read from that day.

A display of work done in the class is of interest to staff as well as other patients. Staff members report that they see individuals in an entirely different way after reading their written work. An assignment which makes a good display is based on brightly colored pictures collected by the teacher. After each student chooses one he would like to write about, the teacher mounts it on paper and types the piece on the same sheet in a pleasing arrangement. Choosing a picture is fun and sometimes more than one person writes about the same picture, producing entirely different stories, adding to the interest.

Variety adds interest to assignments based on objects. A collection of things in the middle of the table never fails to stimulate writing. It is poignant to realize that the domestic clutter patients had in their homes—in basements and attics—is no longer part of their world. A garden hoe or a canning jar is fun to see.

If the assembled things are chosen around a theme, the first few minutes of the class can be spent discovering the theme. A summer display, for example, might include a canning funnel, sea shells, sun glasses, fly swatter, fishing tackle, berry baskets, hoe, and a handful of soil. After the general theme of summer is discovered, each writer may choose one object to write about. The freedom to choose among the objects leads the writer to think about what he wants to emphasize. There is no "right" story.

* * *

Our business in life is not to get ahead of other people, but to get ahead of ourselves.

—*Maltie B. Babcock*

* * *

After about twenty minutes of writing and interviewing each writer reads what he has written, with the teacher reading the results of interviews. The group may be led to note differences and similarities, the developing style of the individual writer, places where more information would be interesting, or possible uses of the material in contests or publications. Appreciation of and interest in each others' work is keen. When one writer won a prize in a statewide writing contest, the whole home celebrated.

Some writers will ask for an assignment to do during the week. These manuscripts should be read in class as well. The more involved students benefit from editorial suggestions from the teacher.

Holidays and other special events are obvious subjects for writing. The nursing home newsletter editor is always pleased to have pieces on these subjects. Since the writing must be done well before the holiday, it is fun to celebrate in the writing class a month early. A small branch of pine given to every member of the class in November produced many Christmas stories, but some that were not about Christmas as well. The poem at the beginning of this chapter is an example. The branches were carefully taken back to the participants' rooms and put into vases. Again we are reminded of little things that matter so much when you no longer have them and how this enhanced appreciation adds to writing.

THE SUCCESSFUL TEACHER

Teachers who have worked successfully in nursing homes admit that it is hard work. They must concentrate and be aware of each person in the group in a way that is not required in the usual teaching setting. There are special problems that require creative solutions. Individuals who cannot seem to attend as their fellow class members talk or read may find it possible to be still if the teacher quietly walks to them and puts a hand on shoulder or hand. Indeed gentle touching comes naturally to the teacher who gets along well with nursing home residents.

Another special problem involves the individual who never stops talking. The firm reminder that it is a writing, not talking class, coupled with an invitation to the individual to write, takes the attention away from the talking to the alternative. Indeed such individuals may be well focused in writing and, in time, they will find that writing helps them not to repeat themselves in speech.

If the job is hard and demanding of creative solutions it also offers extraordinary job satisfaction. The teacher can see progress where expectations are not high and comes to know the transcendent spirits of the students as they rise above their plights through writing. It is a maturing experience to know such people and to learn from them that life is worth living all of one's life.

* * *

The winter is over and gone. The time of singing is come and the voice of the turtle is heard in our land.

—Song of Solomon

FUNDING FOR CLASSES

Until one class demonstrates its value, funding for classes in nursing homes may be difficult to find. Once administrators, families, and governmental officials see the results they are likely to speak with pride that such classes exist. Perhaps they, too, begin to lose their fear of nursing homes.

Unless they are put into the position of competing for funds with the program, the staunchest allies of the programs are nursing home staff. Some regular staff members may want to teach such classes themselves or find outside people to come in for a limited time. A community organization of artists who provide the classes is ideal. In advocating support for such an organization one older member of a commission on aging remarked that the Older Americans Act was not intended to keep people from starving, it was designed to enrich the lives of older people.

As students give readings for civic groups, publish in local papers, win prizes, read over radio, and give their work to family and friends, support for such programs grows. The citizenry is educated about old age through their writings and begin to think about their own inevitable time of being old. It's a wonderful thing to have something to look forward to *always*.

Chapter 7

A Day's Plan
With Lesson Outlines

It is much easier to improvise if you have a plan. This seeming paradox is at the heart of creative teaching. Written lesson plans and assembled materials take a great deal of pressure off the teacher who is not rigid in following in every detail the plan in front of him. Indeed, an overly rigid teacher will probably not be comfortable with classes of older people, plan or not.

The plans outlined here have been used and they work. They are flexible and take into account the special limitations and opportunities offered by particular class settings.

Chapter Six gives a day's plan for classes in the nursing home setting. One plan at the end of the chapter is adapted for nursing home use, indicating how others may also be adapted following the principles outlined in the chapter.

ANNOUNCEMENTS

Older people seem not to be impatient with the inevitable announcements which may irritate the teacher. On the contrary, they carefully record dates and directions. These may include times and places for classes and field trips, writing events and contests, successes by class members, radio programs and magazine articles of interest to writers, as well as messages required by center or nursing home staff.

* * *

Images are the straws from which I make my bricks.

—Muriel Spark

An in-class writing exercise commands the full attention of Marion Nereim and C. George Extrom. Photo by Karen Updike.

THE IN-CLASS WRITING EXERCISE

Before a musician, actor or athlete performs, he warms up his instrument, his voice, his muscles. He does not start cold; he starts when he is in the swing of things, in the groove, his adrenalin flowing. He must be psyched up for the performance, so that *it* may be the peak, and not just a prelude to a finer job later, when it doesn't count. Think of the in-class writing exercise as this kind of warm-up for a writer. What he is warming up is his capacity to think and feel in images from his own personal experience rather than in small talk conventions and generalities. He is also physically putting himself in the position and posture of writing, moving a pen across paper with no possibility of procrastinating or evading the subject. In this way he demonstrates to himself that the poem or story is in the pen, and not in the head; in other words, one can only write by writing. One cannot want to write, hope to write some day, have a zillion ideas to write. One must actually push a pen across a pad of paper to be a writer. This certainty is what someone meant when he said, ''A writer writes with his hands.'' Senior center staff in one rural community cautioned one teacher that above all, members of the group would want to make, see, and have a finished product. They were accustomed to quilting, canning, and cooking vast quantities for church suppers. When they got together, they wanted to see results. Our classes would be suspect if we just wallowed in wonderful words and good feelings and did not come up with some sort of product. Yet any writer knows the panic of the empty page before him, the enforced solitude one must seek in order to be able to work. Warming up a faculty such as one's sharp sensory perceptions by writing first within the support of a group had much merit.

* * *

A creative writing class may be one of the last places you can go where your life still matters. Your life matters, all right. It is all you've got for sure, and without it you are dead.

—Richard Hugo

* * *

Initially we called them ''finger exercises,'' a term we borrowed from musicians. For eight or ten meetings we based the in-class exercise on one of the five senses, and asked that they merely make lists of images during the ten minutes allotted for this exercise. List your favorite smells or your most detested smells, and tell briefly about them. List your favorite brown things, your favorite feels, or the sounds you hear when it is so quiet one can really hear the smallest thing. After about four meetings we suggest they write in sentences, not just lists. The topics chosen continue to evoke powerful sensory images: Tell of paths you have walked, bells you remember hearing, flowers that remind you of people, popular songs you will always associate with certain events. It is best to have the in-class exercise set up or dovetail with the writing assignment for the week. In this way people leave class with the comfortable feeling of having made a start.

For the in-class exercise we make it clear that writers are not to sit about thinking and chewing their pencils. They are to write even if what they write is that we are tyrants for saying they must write. Once a teacher asked a class to set short warm-up exercises for themselves each day at home. A woman came back to report that she had set the stove timer for ten minutes all right, but when it went off, she was so deeply in concentration that it scared her half to death, causing a great jagged pen scratch across the paper when she jumped. She had taken our request that each exercise be *at least* ten minutes in duration to mean that it could be *only* ten minutes long. Actually if the at home exercises somehow convinced participants of the value of daily writing periods, and if they continued them uninterrupted more often in the future, we would be delighted.

After the group has wound up their exercise, ask, but do not insist, that they read them to one another. Find a humorous, light-hearted way to ban all their protestations of "This is not very good," or "not as good," or "I didn't quite get what you meant, but, well, anyway, here goes." Suggest that the class listen with pencils poised to make notes on things they like so that they have something favorable to comment upon after the reading. Hearing each person read is a good way to reinforce how much they do have to write about. Some teachers call it a time of pump priming. The teacher might say, "I'd like to hear more about that," or "sounds to me like you could write pages about that corn crib." It is also an opportunity for the teacher to explain certain devices with examples supplied by the students themselves.

The in-class exercise serves to bolster confidence, acquaint group members with each other's work, model journal writing techniques, get them started on the weekly writing idea, and initiate them gently into the art of giving kind, but helpful, criticism. Most important of all, it inundates the class with images to remember, notice, and enjoy and subtly underscores how much they contribute to clear, engaging writing.

* * *

Death is a power like any other pull of the earth . . .
There is almost nothing that does not signal loneliness,
then loveliness, then something connecting all we will become.

—"In Passing," Stanley Plumly

RESPONDING TO ASSIGNMENTS READ ALOUD IN CLASS

Much as they wish to be heard, older adults are initially timid about reading their own work. Listen with a pencil in your hand to make quick notes of specific things you can comment favorably on after the reading—a strong verb, a vivid image, evidence of an authentic, genuine voice, evidence of controlling and manipulating the material artistically to change what really happened into something more exciting or powerful. One teacher remembers feeling so ill at ease when she first began meeting with older adults about writing that she made up a list of adjectives she could use to respond in a generally favorable manner to their work lest she became tongue-tied and could not think of a thing to say. She never used that infamous and fear-inspired crutch. Fortunately she had the presence of mind and the regard for them to do the hard work of real listening to their writing.

Beginning writers fear they will reveal too much of themselves in their work. Consequently they choose safe topics and idealize their past experiences. The result is phony, sentimental, unauthentic writing which should not be admired or encouraged. Instead the teacher should try to ferret out from what is written what might really be important to that writer and make for a better piece of writing.

Another obsession of beginning writers is to be honest and tell it just as it really was or is. They insist upon this even while unconsciously idealizing action and character in the extreme. Nothing could be more boring or unrewarding to hear; do not distinguish it by much interest or comment. Instead, cite the one place (hopefully there is one) in which he has written well, and wax enthusiastic over it. Value it, enjoy it, hold it up, for the class to gaze at, savour, and admire, even if it is the only felicitous phrase embedded in an otherwise muddy matrix. In this way you will be operationally setting standards for genuine, powerful writing.

A second reason for listening to their work in class is to help them mine from it other subjects to write about that might be even more powerful subjects for them. Should a student grow excited about another's subject, take time to track down with him what it is he could write about in this area.

Use the pieces read as teaching material. As a group, find a better title for one, suggest a different starting place for another, question how clear the motivation was for a third, discuss the effectiveness of dialogue in another. Different works will present different problems to illustrate techniques to the entire class. Save editorial suggestions on sentence structure and syntax for written comments later when you have the manuscript in your hands.

Even when the student is telling a story he has not yet written, it is effective to stop him and repeat a phrase he has used if it is good, to call attention to it and highlight it. "You just said, 'You know, a carp will climb!' That sounds just like you. That is your voice. Keep it. Don't try to write another person's fishing idyl. Saying it your way is best."

* * *

Poetry is a way of looking at something longer than it will last.

—*Unknown*

* * *

Our best response to a writer's work is to take the trouble to really listen to it, for then no matter what we say, he will feel valued, and feeling valued, he will begin to say more significant things in more interesting ways, producing better and better material to share.

THE BREAK

Time goes quickly when a writing class is underway. Concentration becomes intense as participants respond to assigned exercises, listen to each other's manuscripts, and verbalize their reactions. Two hours hardly seem enough, especially to the teacher who wants to tell about resources and give direct instruction in addition to the critiqueing workshop. It is tempting to keep the group going nonstop for the two hours, to insure the inclusion of all planned activities. This is not a good idea. A break is important, even though it may require a paring down of the day's schedule.

Older people need to move about periodically to relieve chair-cramped muscles and aid blood circulation. Some welcome the chance to visit rest rooms. They enjoy refreshing themselves with a cup of coffee or tea.

Most want the opportunity, however brief, to talk as individuals. As in any group, their social interest in each other is keen. Furthermore, those who have private concerns about writing appreciate a chance to confer with the teacher.

If a volunteer from the class has put a pot of water on to heat before class and coffee, tea, and chocolate are provided, the break can be taken when it works out best. Some classes want to simply leave the table and get their refreshments whenever the individual chooses, but if no one has gone at about the halfway point, the teacher should pause.

Occasionally the break becomes a celebration of a birthday or some other special event. Sometimes it inspires a writer as evidenced by the following poem.

The Break

If you happen to ask me
What can you do
Gladly and proudly
I would tell you.

Milk a cow, drive a tractor
Paint my house, type a chapter,
Play the organ, grow some seeds,
Use a shovel, pull some weeds.

When you ask me
     for free verse
Everything
     seems worse and worse.
And so, dear friends, to remove the taste
     of this painful rhyme, I offer in lieu
Toll House cookies to you!

—Carolyn Every
for coffee break from writing class

INSTRUCTIONAL RESOURCES

One teacher, conscious of how little older people used the city library, tried to make a point of having everyone visit it. She pushed very hard for such participation. One day one of the men in her class made the following report to the class,

> I went to the library, just like the teacher so strongly advised. I went straight to the information desk, as she advised, and asked where the men's room was. I was told it was right

down the hall and when I got there I heard strange noises in the next stall. There were feet protruding from the stall with toes turned up. I went back to the front desk and told the librarian there was a man in the men's room on the floor with his toes turned up. She said there was another men's room on the second floor.

The hapless teacher never knew whether this was true or apocryphal but she learned not to overdo selling resources. Easy does it.

The libraries with their branches, buses, large print books, writer's markets and magazines, art and music resources, and friendly librarians are, of course, wonderfully helpful to the writer. Even in rural areas library services are usually available today. The teacher will need to be well informed about such services.

Writer's groups, from professional journalism clubs to freelancers' round robins, will be interested in hearing about your classes and eager to welcome your "graduates."

Church and service groups, radio stations, TV stations, schools, and others make use of program material. Your students will be able to give interesting readings after they get started in writing.

For non-fiction writing, interviews offer a rich source of material. People in the community will be very willing to be interviewed and written about by members of the class.

When specific writing problems of grammar, punctuation, and syntax seem to be the same for nearly everyone in the class, a discussion of the particular problem is in order. *The Elements of Style* by Strunk and White is the best general reference. Students often buy this book and read it many times. *The Christian Science Monitor* offers a pamphlet on how to improve writing which is inexpensive when ordered in quantity. *Poetry handbook* by Babette Deutsch is an invaluable aid in finding answers about poetry.

Reading from fine literature with attention drawn to structure and content is a classroom resource that is not only fun but helpful to the writer. This may also lead members of the group to read more widely than they had previously done. A sample list of books is in the back of this book.

The daily newspaper, periodicals, even advertisements which you see every day provide excellent examples of writing and material which can be used to provoke other writing. How-to articles, for example, are usually short and look easy to write. A class that tries to write them soon finds that they are not so easy and will enjoy examining examples for technique. Everything they read is more interesting when they are aware of how it was written.

When requests for resource material begin to come from the class, don't be afraid to say you don't know where to find it, but always try to help the student find what he needs. Literary resources are more helpful if they are related to the assignment for the day. For example, poems by Amy Lowell and William Carlos Williams might be brought if the assignment has to do with imagist poems. A list of photographers willing to be interviewed would be helpful if a non-fiction article about cameras is the assignment.

A seemingly endless supply of resources seems to materialize as you go along and come to understand the situation in which your students find themselves. The simple fact that most older adults no longer have extensive storage space limits the resources available to them.

* * *

not loving life enough
to grieve, we circle back into the dark.
Your sister paints in order to forget
that nothing lasts

—*"Making Her Will," Robert Pack*

* * *

MARKETING

Some members of every class of older writers, and all of some classes, will be interested in selling what they write. For some, this will mean continuing to do as they have before and for others it will mean selling in a different market. But for most it will be a new experience.

If manuscripts are to be submitted for publication, they must be prepared in the prescribed manner. Several good references for this purpose are listed in Resources at the back of this book.

Deciding to send material to an editor involves deciding to accept rejection slips as part of the territory. One way to ease the writer through their arrival is to keep all material, including all drafts related to a written piece in a used manila envelope or folder with pockets. On the outside list ten markets with the dates of submission and return noted. This helps the writer to immediately send the manuscript out again. After ten rejections a rewrite may be in order. Most writers admit this with a chuckle.

Finding the right market for a given piece of writing involves, first and always, reading the magazines and newspapers in which you wish to publish. Quick surveys at news stands help but thorough reading in libraries is better. The library also provides *The Writer's Market,* a reference work published yearly which lists markets by type of writing. *The Writer* and *Writer's Digest* magazines also list markets. Many older writers enjoy the articles in these magazines as well. For beginning writers, *The Writer* is probably the more easily read of the two magazines.

Photocopied pages of market lists chosen by the teacher for a particular piece of writing will illustrate to the student what is needed. In addition, the teacher who has become market conscious may be able to make suggestions when reading students' work. Knowing the local market is especially important and listings of such publications are rarely available. Small shopping papers, tourist material, hometown newspapers, and historical society publications all use freelance memory pieces, for example.

There are newsletters published by countless groups who regularly look for relevant writing. These range from environmental groups to medical problem support groups such as the Alzheimer's newsletter. Poetry and inspirational writing by people who have cared for victims or who have themselves experienced illness is always needed. Church bulletins and devotional publications appeal to some older writers as places where they would like to be published. There is a Christian Writers' Market published each year. Publishers such as David C. Cook are constantly seeking well-written devotional work.

When most of the people in a class are interested in publishing, class time may be used to discuss it. If only a few are interested, the break may be utilized for individual conferences and a short time after class may be needed as well. Written suggestions by the teacher usually need to be followed up with a conversation with the writer.

Sometimes a student embarks upon a long writing project such as a book about barns in his state or a collection of short stories or family anecdotes. The teacher may play a coach-like role with such writers, encouraging and editing. Such students will simply enroll every term, often with the same teacher. We have seen this happen with dramatic and proud results.

While many older writers are eager to publish their work, they also take great interest and pleasure in seeing their fellow writers published. We have not seen competitiveness as a problem among older writers. The teacher, must, of course, be sensitive to spending a disproportionate amount of class time on one person's work.

There are many rewards for writing. Publication is only one and, for the older writer, it is often not the most important. But for the ones who are dedicated and determined enough to publish, it gives great satisfaction.

FORM AND STRUCTURE

Writing forms are many. If you want to cover examples of each form from each age of writing or to cover all of the criticism ever written of the form, then a lifetime is needed. If, on the other hand, you want to learn enough to practice the forms for yourself and do selective reading, they can be enormously stimulating.

At the outset of each class term, state simply that you will try to discover what it is each person wants to write and help him decide what form best suits the material. Following each exercise to awaken memory and creative thought, offer a different writing form to be put into the writer's bag of tricks and taken out when needed. Family jokes may become reminiscence articles, eulogies may become poems, and sermons, essays.

The Japanese three line poem (haiku) may help to focus a rambling commentary and, strangely, the more complicated forms, for some people, tend to free the emotions. For example, the assignment of a villanelle, a complex rhymed poetry form, helped some previously uptight people to put their real feelings into writing. Perhaps this is freedom through discipline. The same assignment led to one of the most interesting dialogues in writing that the teacher had encountered. Dylan Thomas' "Do Not Go Gentle Into That Good Night" was used as an example of the villanelle. Older people protested that Thomas was a young man writing about age; an older writer would not view death that way. But one woman wrote: "You are all wrong. I intend to rage all the way." Rage, justified or not, could be expressed in an acceptable way among writing friends. It seems likely that the discipline of the poem's structure was necessary to elicit this response.

Written on the Shore

My life is like a shoreline
A host to every tide.
When I depart will it reveal
Scenes frought with shame or pride?

No sign of friendly footprints
Of guests who didn't stay,
Or will the sand be furrowed
With paths from every way?

Are stones all dull and mossy
My will to win dismayed?
Or were those tides conscripted
To be harnessed and enslaved?

Did drift wood seek this haven
To share my slothful hours
Or does my shore look ready
To cope with any powers?

When I depart my shoreline
May strangers look and say,
"Whoever lived his life here
Made the most of every day."

                     —Julian Clark

Castles

As the waters claimed the castles
that were built along the shore,
Poe's midnight quoting raven
seemed to echo, "Nevermore."

Nevermore will those sand castles
line the shore another day,
for the dreams revealed in each one
have been forever washed away.

But dream castles, mind created,
need not fear the creeping tide,
for in the haven of a fantasy
they have a place to hide.

So if my castles fragment
and crumble in the air,
I fear not the raven's warning,
for I know more dreams are there.

—Leone Callahan

A Memory

I remember well those hills, the trees,
These dreams that take my breath away,
White Birches trembling in the breeze.

Blue water sparkling through the leas
I wandered where the grasses sway.
I remember well those hills, the trees,

Whose presence, from each mortal, frees
Old cares of every tiring day.
White Birches trembling in the breeze.

Winds softly undulating as they please
Make ripples in the waves of hay;
I remember well those hills, the trees.

With sharpened clarity the mind's eye sees,
These scenes in fallow mem'ry lay,
White Birches trembling in the breeze.

From feebled brain the picture flees
But not from mine, ah God, I pray—
I remember well those hills, the trees,
White Birches trembling in the breeze.

—Mary Brodzeller
Courtesy of *Heartland Journal*

Do Just What the Doctor Sez
(reflections on a personal experience)

"I'll tell you what has caused your pain:
A great big blood clot in your vein.
I'll have to put you on bed rest
With one foot higher than your chest."
(A funny way to sleep at night!
But doctors always know what's right.)

"You'll have to take this Warfarin,
It helps to make your blood more thin."
(I didn't think that sounded nice.
I'd always heard 'twas used for mice.)

(It certainly did work for me—
It soon caused fluid on my knee!)
"For that the best thing I have tried
Is hydro-chloro-thia-zide."
(But what I later came to know:
It also makes blood pressure low.)
"Now that we got your blood too thin
You must omit the Coumadin.
Wear this stretch sock from thigh to toe
And keep it on each place you go."

"You should swim often at the Y"
(How can I keep my stretch sock dry?)
Walk vigorously to distant points.
Avoid weight bearing on your joints.
How do all this he didn't say,
But finally I learned the way.
In spite of seeming contradiction
He pulled me back to prime condition.
The doctor's orders do make sense
If follow'd in the right sequence!

—Fred M. Smith
Courtesy *Heartland Journal*

That is not to say, of course, that free verse is easy to write or that it has no form. It is a very useful form for classes with the aging. They may reject it out of hand and accept it only when reminded of "old" free verse examples such as the poetry of Milton or Whitman. Free verse may also be approached through subject matter. Muriel Rukheyser's "Girl With the Scissors" evokes deep feelings among people who have known economic depression and unemployment. It is at once clear that this poem could not have been written in rhyme.

Another way to approach free verse is through the various techniques used within the form. For example, an imagist poet, such as Amy Lowell, uses very different techniques from a narrative poet such as Longfellow in "Hiawatha" or Frost in "The Hired Man."

To approach form in prose, writing the article, with all its variations, is an easy beginning. The very factual, although difficult to write, how-to article is an interesting way to start. It may produce sewing or cooking directions, or how to use the local bus, but it may also give a forum for people to tell about their professional skills. A former accountant with the state office of taxation wrote about how to fill out income averaging tax forms, and a former pastor how to answer questions asked by grandchildren.

Interview articles may be based on interviews with each other in class or on going into the community to find interesting subjects. These interviews may be done by phone for those unable to get out or they may be interviews with a doctor, therapist, or janitor where the writer lives. Thinking ahead about what to ask in an interview helps the writer focus his thoughts in other settings. Identifying himself as a writer to another person whom he is interviewing is hard at first, but is remarkably self-affirming. People like to talk to writers and they like to talk about themselves, facts older writers soon learn.

Humorous and reminiscence articles lead naturally into essay and opinion writing; comparing the past with how things are now brings philosophical observations. Letters to the editor often grow out of writing brought to class, as do short pieces for church or club publications. Critical writing about plays or concerts others in the group have also attended has led to more than one after class get-together. An inclination towards extreme optimism and cloying sweetness is likely to elicit gentle teasing which is far more effective in helping the writer overcome his lack of realism than sour put-downs. People often see in writing what they do not recognize in their conversation.

Individual style and preference will, of course, play an important part in what forms the individual writer will choose to work in, but suggesting a new form often makes ideas fall into place so that they can be written. Writing in a different form is just one more tool for the fertile minds of the aging as they continue to surprise and delight themselves and others.

THE HOME ASSIGNMENT

The weekly assignment is essential to a student's development as a writer. While listening and critiquing lead to insight and improvement, these in-class activities are properly viewed as supplementary to the work done outside the class. Not even the in-class writing exercise is adequate exposure to the writing process. A developing writer must grapple with a variety of themes and forms, pursuing these under circumstances which offer maximum opportunity to think and practice without interruption. One must expect and allow time for false starts and changes in direction. Revising and rewriting are necessary. It takes time—often in multiple segments—to prepare even a first draft which might satisfy the writer and his class critics. While the group can be a wonderful reinforcer and enriching agent, it can offer no substitute for solitary hard work at the writing desk.

A teacher must give careful thought to the range, quality, and sequence of outside tasks. Planning will be guided by awareness of what the students have already done, what their apparent needs are, their interests, and the range of criterion-based goals the teacher brings to the class. Writers who teach will tend to emphasize the topics and forms with which they are most comfortable. The number of class meetings, hence the number of opportunities to make assignments, will certainly play a role. Pre-determined priorities should be flexible because changes are likely to become appropriate as the group progresses. In deciding what the home writing experiences should be, the teacher moves from simple to more complex tasks in a logical progression.

After deciding upon an assignment, the teacher must schedule the introduction of that assignment in the day's agenda. The point during class when that introduction occurs will vary with differing styles of teaching, but the options are worth mentioning. Perhaps the most obvious time to announce the assignment is at the end of the session. Just before leaving for the day, the teacher explains what should be done at home prior to the next meeting. Another possibility exists when the assignment relates directly to an activity which occurs early in the session. For example, the in-class exercise might serve as advance exposure to some task the teacher wants the students to develop further at home. Thus the group may write in class about a photograph provided by the teacher and, as follow-up, individuals are assigned to write about photographs in their own possession at home which have meaning in their lives. A logical time to present this would be immediately after the photograph exercise which might be first on the class agenda. Similarly, an assignment to try writing haiku at home might follow a description in class of the structure and principles of haiku writing—an instructional activity appearing midway, perhaps, in the class. Assignments may be given routinely at the same point in the agenda or they may vary to fit the timing of related activities.

While assignments are essential to the teaching of writing, flexibility is desirable in assignments. Some students may not be able to generate excitement about one or more of the tasks the teacher has in mind for the class. Perhaps they have done them before, perhaps some intervening event or ongoing situation competes for the student's attention, or perhaps they have reached a point in their writing in which assignments are self-generating. For such students, it is more important that *some* assignment be done and less important that it be the teacher's group assignment.

TEACHER FOLLOW-UP TO WEEK'S LESSON

Much more usually occurs during the two hour class period than one had anticipated in the lesson plan. In fact some weeks after class the original lesson plan may seem to have been meant for some other class. It is important for us to be able to set aside our plans to avail ourselves of fortuitous teaching moments as writers read their work. Ideas for future writing assignments for the class as a whole, technical points it is clear they all simply must know, are bound to occur to the teacher while the class is in progress. Just the right book or poem one student must see might pop into your mind, if you could only remember to bring her the book next time. For easy access, it is wise to make notes to yourself about these and other matters around the margins of the lesson plan itself, or on the space left beneath it. Try to keep these notes separate from your jottings on student readings.

Be sure to note who has not read and let them start first the next time if you are unable to hear everyone's work each time. Sometimes discussions simply grow too long, or the works read are too long to accommodate everybody. Promise them they will begin next time before they leave class, then write it down and do it. Nothing is more important than having students' work read and read frequently. Older adults may take umbrage at apparent over-sights.

LESSON PLANS

The lesson plans which follow are examples and may be used in any desired order.

*In literature it is our business to give people the thing that will
make them say: "oh yes I know what you mean." It is never to
tell them something they don't know, but something they know
and hadn't thought of saying. It must be something they recognize.*

—*Robert Frost*

* * *

LESSON PLAN: BOXES

Purpose

To stimulate memory and imagination by displaying a variety of
boxes, one of which will actually contain something.

Discussion

Do you like boxes? Do you save them? What can you tell by the
shape? If you were going to give one of these to the person on your
right which would you choose? Why? Can you tell which one con-
tains refreshments?

Writing Exercise

Write about one of the boxes on the table. Make up what is in it
and who it is for. Or write about a similar one you once opened.

Read Resulting Manuscripts

Each person reads his own, if possible. Those interviewed will
have theirs read by the teacher or another student. Ask each time
whether a piece is memory or imagination. Finish with home work
brought in from room-bound students or students doing extra work.

Conclusion

Open every box, finishing with one containing crackers to be
served. This should be elaborately disguised.

Homework Assignment (Optional)

Write about something that is not what it appears to be.*

Reading From Literature

"The Gift" by O. Henry, "Apartment House" by Gerald Raftery in *A Gift of Watermelon Pickle,* poetry anthology, Lothrop, Lee, & Shepard.

Boxes

The velvet box holds a necklace
  with a gold cross
  for a secret someone.
The long box holds candles
  white, for church.
The red box holds a soft white scarf
  for the girl in church.
I would go with her
and her mother. She
has MS like me. I
still pray for her.

—Phil

Boxes

Boxes, for me, remain dull, rectangular or square, composed of wood, various metals, plastics or cardboard. They are needed to protect contents from rough handling from points of origin to destination. I have been vitally interested in cartons used in shipping the many kinds of meat products through the country by Oscar Mayer & Co.

I have visited the draymen at the many destinations to observe our shipments as to the condition of the cartons, refrigeration, and the drayman's operation. Especially we pressed the ever present need for refrigeration of our perishable product.

In 1945 we were shipping most of our products by wet ice refrigerator cars with a fleet of 500 cars. Gradually, because

---

*Some members will leave but others may enjoy a half hour to an hour of reading.

of faster in transit time and mechanical refrigeration, we got rid of our fleet and shipped via trucks to all points. Both railroad cars and semi-trucks carry minimum weight of 30,000 to 40,000 lbs. and can be classified as big boxes on wheels.

The customer pays for the cost of the box but the cost is included in the final price of the product.

The word box is used in other ways. Baseball has a batter's box, a pitcher's box, a manager's box, coach's box, and umpire's box. Knitting and crocheting have box squares and a person may say that he is boxed in, meaning that he is covered on all sides. "I'll box your ears" means that someone is due for a cuffing.

Houses, apartment buildings, and office buildings may be classified as compartmentalized boxes. The architects and engineers who plan these compartments need some creativeness and feeling for design as well as being accomplished in drafting. This nursing home is basically a box.

We all take a box or carton for granted because it covers up or encloses the main object. But it keeps its dullness intact throughout.

—Doc

LESSON PLAN: SPECIAL OCCASIONS

Purpose

The celebration of special occasions, both personal and community related, is important in the lives of older people just as it is for younger ones, perhaps more so. These events are nice to remember and to anticipate. To be able to make a memorable written contribution on such an occasion feels good. This exercise is designed to make that possible.

Exercise

Think about a very special occasion that was important in your life. List ways in which writing helped to make it special. Did you get letters? Did anyone write a poem? Did anyone prepare jokes or stories?

Write down a special event which is coming that will be important to someone you know. What kind of writing might make it more memorable?

Reading of Exercise Results

Discuss ideas and encourage suggestions.

Resources

1. *Free verse.* This is poetry that has the sound of poetry and the cadences of speech but it is not rhymed or metered. Walt Whitman wrote such poetry. Listen to "When Lilacs First in the Dooryard Bloomed" which honors President Lincoln. "Olaf Hougen Was Eighty-five Last Night" by Lenore M. Coberly is a contemporary poem honoring an engineer but it may also be read as honoring all teachers and the teaching profession.

2. *Nostalgic fillers.* These are often used by newspapers and magazines to fill small spaces; hence the name. But they are also nice to nice to put into a remembrance book for someone who is being honored on an anniversary, retirement, or promotion. The story should be told with colorful detail but unnecessary detail must be ruthlessly cut. Your classmates can help you detect unnecessary words when you read next week. Any issue of *Readers Digest* is rich with examples.

3. *Limericks.* This is a poetry form used in fun. Sometimes it is used to ridicule and shame but it is also used to tell a joke or make a remark that is much funnier when rhymed. *Primipara* poetry journal, Fall-Winter, 1980-81 has good examples. Many books of limericks will be found in the library.

Break

Reading Material Written Since Last Week

It is important to jot down your comments as the piece is being read. It is easy to forget what they were. We will not be criticizing or commenting upon what the writer is writing about, only upon whether he has succeeded in doing what he wished to do. Listen carefully for especially well-turned phrases or descriptive verbs and nouns. Yes, descriptive!

Assignment

Write a very short story or filler or a poem in free verse or limerick form for the special occasion you thought of during the exercise.

Sabina

Reading to the children
Baking bread and cookies
Always there. This loving woman.
When did she wear the flapper dress?
Black chiffon and flounce?
Jacket lined with embroidered roses?
Buttoned in jet.
Satin pumps.
When did she carry the beaded bag
dangling from its golden chain?
Did she slither into some convertible?
Or just sashay
down the street?
Who gave her the faded corsage
pressed for half a century in
the family bible?
A lad in white flannels?
The grocer's delivery boy
stiff and shy in a dark blue suit?
Did they kiss her?
Did they love her?
Why did she never tell?
Why did I never ask?

—Jo Lynaugh
Courtesy of *Heartland Journal*

The Fourth of July

When I was a boy the Fourth of July was one of the most important days of the summer. After school was out we boys would save our money and try to find some jobs to earn money so we could buy firecrackers, cannon crackers, sparklers, and Roman candles to explode on the Fourth. Of course we had to get some punk too so we could light the fireworks instead of using so many matches. We could hardly wait until it got light enough to get dressed and start waking up the neighborhood by lighting our firecrackers.

I had a brother who was eight years older than I, and he had some six-inchers which I wasn't allowed to have. He put one in our wood hitching post in front of the house and lit it just as the milkman's horse and buggy were passing. The explosion blew the hitching post to smithereens, the horse took off and milk cans spilled in the road for several blocks until somebody managed to stop the horse some distance away.

My father came running out of the house with a switch and gave my brother a good licking. Then he turned to me, shaking the switch, and said, "Let that be a lesson to you!"

—Carl W. Danhouser

The Flag

Today I saw a flag
That swirled its brightness
Against the graying sky

Then thought of flags
The wind whip
Atop the schools

Of other flags
Upon the schoolroom walls
To which we pledged our loyalty

Of penny flags and fireworks
That marked the Fourth
Of each July

Of colors carried on parade
In step
to martial bands

The drab red rag
That flew on merchant ships
Met on an open sea.

Once I saw a thousand flags
That danced across the waves
On craft that cast

An army on the shore
To fight, to die, to triumph
To taste the bitter-sweet
Of Victory.

One day
A flag I shall not see
Will blanket me
That 'tween the crash of rifles
And the bugles plaintive cry
They'll carefully fold and
Give to those I love.

—Benjamin Brothers

Olaf Hougen was Eighty-five Last Night

Olaf Hougen was eighty-five last night.
Years, of course, not feet.
Although, among the bowed shadows of students
in that candle lit room, he seemed that tall.

Oh, some stood higher, richer,
but they had learned from him
to look clear-eyed unafraid at greatness
and to know which way was up.

Simple accolades and laughter
that remembered only the times between
problems unsolved at midnight
seemed to confound him.

As he rose and faced the praise
he saw Japan, Texas, Norway,
microbiology, thermodynamics, theology and time
in the faces of those he had taught.

Leaning forward, we waited for him to say
something quotable, sentimental, gay—
something we could later relay
linking ourselves with his special day.

But he lifted us out of ourselves
into the place where an honest man
looks straight at the way things are
and sums them up as an engineer can.

He begged us to take note of the colleague
who never had gone far away
as others, privileged, had done.
He only stayed and made things run.

He asked us to remember another teacher
who taught less glamorous stuff
like how to keep your eyesight
in a chemical engineering lab.

Those were the men, Olaf said,
who were remembered at last
by wandering, wondering students
in the grasping, blinding world of work.

Remember? Remember—
he asked for a calculation of
the height of a gas absorption column.
The student put on the board precisely
one hundred and seven and three-tenths feet.
Hougen's single comment was,
"I certainly would hang onto
that three-tenths of a foot."

The teacher was eighty-five last night.
Years, of course, not feet.
Although, among the bowed shadows of students
in that candle lit room, he seemed that tall.

—Lenore M. Coberly
Reprinted by permission *Chemical Engineering Progress*

LESSON PLAN: A PINE BOUGH

Purpose

A single object looked at in different ways may evoke very different memories. It may bring a memory that seems not related to the object itself but which begs to be written down. Having every class member write about the same object makes hearing the resulting work very interesting. They will all be different no matter what the object is, but it helps to choose one that can be experienced easily in several ways.

Exercise

Give each person a pine branch. Rub hands over it, smell it, hold it upright and look at it; look at it lying on the table, look through it toward a light, wave it through the air, blow into its needles, and spend a few minutes privately with it.

In ten minutes write about one thing you thought of while considering the pine branch.

Reading to the Class

Watch for words which make you see, smell, or feel the pine branch in a new way. Watch for words that you have often heard before in writing or speaking about pine.

Resources

The Nostalgic Article is one of the most often published of nonfiction articles. The feature section of almost any Sunday paper will have remembering stories on subjects ranging from Thanksgiving on the farm to going from coast to coast in a Model T. Children like stories of times past. Good examples of reminiscence or nostalgic writing are "Bobolinka's Neighbor" *Vanity Fair,* May, 1983 by Diana Trilling and *Soup,* a children's book by Robert Newton Peck, Yearling Book, Dell Publishing Co., 1974.

Break

Reading Material Written Outside of Class

Assignment

Write a reminiscence article about the time you remembered while you studied the pine bough. Remember that the haiku poem may be about pine and that free verse poems can tell a story.

First Love

We stroll
Beneath
The moonlit pines
Where fallen needles

Soften every sound
Save that of
Windharps overhead
Clasp hands
Shyly kiss
Pledge love
Forevermore.

Forevermore
Each day
Drops like needles
To the ground
And stills
The love
That blows
Upon the windharps
Of my memory.

—Benjamin Brothers

LESSON PLAN: BODY PARTS

Purpose

To promote use of body images in writing. Elderly writers who share this kind of personal information are likely to do so with candor and humor. Thus humorous writing can be a prime focus.

In-class Exercise

Ask the students to make a list of words which would describe their own bodies starting with childhood and continuing to the present. Individuals share their lists orally.

Home Assignment

Instruct the students as follows: choose a specific body part (your own) and write about it. Try using the essay form in your composition. Assume the essay to be "a short literary composition in prose presenting an analytic or interpretative treatment of a single topic or theme from a limited or personal point of view" (from *The Essay: Subjects and Stances*). Other forms are acceptable, if preferred.

Resources

Benchley, Robert, "My Face" (essay)
Coleridge, Mary Elizabeth, "Eyes" (poem)
Crane, Stephen, "The Heart" (poem)
Dickinson, Emily, "The Brain is Wider Than the Sky" (poem)
Kumin, Maxine, "Song for the Seven Parts of the Body" (poem)
Miller, Vassar, "My Bones Being Wiser" (poem)
Haxton, Brooks, "Tongue" (poem) and "Bones" (poem)
Whitman, Walt, "Faces" (poem)
Williams, C.K., "My Mother's Lips" (poem)
Williams, William Carlos, "Smell!" (poem)

Student Writing

Wattle You Know About That?

The photographer came to our Over/60 Writing Class one afternoon, snapping as he moved about. Kneeling sometimes, standing on a chair, stretching from impossible positions, ever patient, he snapped and snapped.

When the pictures came back there were loud complaints of "all the lousy pictures he'd taken."

Why?

Ballooning chins, turkey necks, wrinkles, pouches, veins, warts, unsightly hairs, scars, seams, large pores, blackheads. Age.

The lens caught us as we truly are. Wattle you know about that?

—Helen I. Klingelhofer

My Face

My eyes are gray green:
cat eyes, they say.
My hair is dark brown
with a few strands of gray.
I've had it lightened,
luminized, they call it,
to soften the lines of my face.

You could call me a plain Jane.
I look better when I smile.

—Gayle Wilkinson

My Voice

"Speak softly," urged grandmama.
"Don't shout," my brother ordered.
"Lower your voice," my folks requested.
    Always, always "modulate that voice."

As long as I remember,
Talking, joking, laughing,
I was cautioned,
    "Modulate that voice."

A high school girl, I tried to curb it,
Stuck a note upon my mirror
written large and clear:
    "Modulate your voice."

College came—the Drama Club
with costumes, prompting, never acting,
still upon my mirror
    "Modulate your voice."

Senior year we cast a play
and I was urged to read the lines.
"You're cast," they cried,
    "The perfect voice."

—Willette McNary

LESSON PLAN: DREAMS

Purpose

To introduce the writer's dream life (night or day) as an appropriate and interesting source of subject matter. Dreams have been called the "royal road to the unconscious"; they can inform the dreamer of his fears, goals, needs, wishes, conflicts and stresses. Recounting a dream can result in a strong prose style, colorful characters, and unusual events. The writer who is always careful to

deal only with known facts and real occurrences may be freed by
dream writing to contact his imaginary realms.

In-class Exercise

Read a guided fantasy to the class, such as "Descend a Dream
Stairway." Participants listen with closed eyes and write after-
wards. Guided fantasies are included in *Thirty Ways to Help You
Write* by Fran Weber Shaw and *The New Diary* by Tristine Rainer.

Home Assignment

Instruct the students as follows: write about one of your own
dreams. You may recount the dream in the present tense as though it
is happening as you write, or you may incorporate it (or some aspect
of it) into another writing form—poem, story, essay or article.

Resources

Berryman, John, *Dream Songs* (poems)
Gardner, Isabella, "Nightmare" (poem)
Healy, Ron, "Dream: Mom and Dad" (poem)
Hughes, Langston, "Dreams" (poem)
Ignatow, David, "The Dream" (poem)
Kumin, Maxine, "The Dreamer, The Dream" and "The Night-
    mare Factory" (poems)
Lipsitz, Lou, "Sleep" (poem)
Rainer, Tristine, "Dream Work" in *The New Diary*
Ridler, Anne, "A Dream Observed" (poem)
Sendak, Maurice, *Where the Wild Things Are* (children's book)
Shine, Frances L., "The Dream Device in Fiction" in *The
    Writer,* February 1980
Simpson, Louis, "I Dreamed That In a City Dark as Paris"
    (poem)
Wendt, Viola, "The Kissed Toad" (poem)

Student Writing

My Dream Friend

I slept and dreamed that life was beauty.
In my dream you were riding

Toward me, all sparkly white
On starlight and moonbeams
Saying, "I want to make you happy
I've come to set you free."
I whispered back on the soft breeze
"Save me from rowing against the wind and tide
Cut the unseen strings that bind me
Give me your warmth, your listening ear
Take the loneliness out of my heart."

I woke to life and duty.
To have such a friend,
I must be such a friend.

—Isabel S. Clark

Vault of Heaven

I struggle . . . reaching . . . groping . . . remembering. I
stand on the marble-like doorsill looking out over the strange
landscape. Red-purple clouds swirl overhead hiding whatever
sky this place has. Or am I being unbearably Earthian in
assuming there is a sky? I try to remember the definition of sky
when I was at home. One, I recall, related to clouds; but there
was another.

Staring out over the perfect undulating green underfoot (they
don't call it ground here) I strive to revive my mind. Why
can't I think? Why don't I remember when I came here or
how? Why are the most simplistic memories gone? I know I
have memories . . . my stomach tells me so.

Ah! The definition I am struggling for flashes across my mind
like a neon sign (now, how did I recall that?). Sky—the vault
of heaven. The firmament. The arch of heaven. Remembrance
struggles on—the sky should be blue, not red-purple, not the
red-purple eddies that swoop so low as to nearly engulf an
unobservant person.

—Eunice Loeb (excerpt from a story)

Dreams

I dream a lot, or so they say,
    though I remember little.

But most of what I know I dream,
turns out to be a riddle.

I rode upon an elephant,
up in the mountains high.

Then swam the mighty ocean,
in the blinking of an eye.

My dreams need destination,
they're too difficult to steer.

Sometimes they lead me forward,
then take me to the rear.

Should David take a moment,
to tell me what they mean,

I'm sure that he would tell me
"It's only just a dream."

—Don Morrick

LESSON PLAN: ANIMALS

Purpose

To try experiencing the world, briefly, from the perspective of a non-human being and putting that experience into words. A writer develops versatility and empathy by writing from many viewpoints. In addition, the choices made taps self-knowledge and reveals something of oneself to the others in the group. Writing for children and doing simple research are introduced as techniques.

In-class Exercise

Ask students (each) to silently choose an animal he or she would like to be. Go around the group (for fun and getting into the spirit of the exercise) asking each to tell which animal he has chosen. Display a variety of animal pictures (a collection large enough to include most of the choices made). Follow this with a timed period of writing, during which each writer "becomes" his animal and writes from that perspective. Share the results orally with comments and discussion by the group.

Home Assignment

Instruct the students as follows: work further with the animal writing you have produced. Options include:

1. Write a story or poem for children in which your animal appears.
2. Return to your human self as the persona and involve yourself in some way with the animal.
3. Do some research and write a factual article about the animal.

Resources

Bishop, Elizabeth, "The Fish" (poem)
Brigham, Bemilr, "The Tiny Baby Lizard" (poem)
Chekhov, Anton, "Boa Constrictor and Rabbit" (story)
Deutsch, Babette, "Lioness Asleep" (poem)
Dickey, James, "The Heaven of Animals" (poem)
Dickinson, Emily, "A Narrow Fellow in the Grass" (poem)
Frost, Robert, "The Runaway" (poem)
Gordon, Arthur, "The Sea Devil" (story)
Haines, John, "If the Owl Calls Again" (poem)
Jeffers, Robinson, "Pelicans" (poem)
Kinnel, Galway, "The Bear" (poem)
Kumin, Maxine, "The Retrieval System" (poem)
Levertov, Denise, "The Snake" (poem)
Lowell, Robert, "Skunk Hour" (poem)
Millay, Edna St. Vincent, "The Buck in the Snow" (poem)
Mitchell, Joni, "Black Crow" (song)
Sward, Robert, "Uncle Dog; The Poet at 9" (poem)
Updike, John, "The Man Who Loved Extinct Mammals" (story)
Whitman, Walt, "Animals" from "Song of Myself" (poem)
Williams, William Carlos, "The Bull" (poem)

Student Writing

Museum Lecture

"I'm a terrible bore," said the dinosaur.
"Talking's such a strain on my brain.
My intelligence quotient is really quite poor,
But I'll try to tell you how life was before.

I was ninety feet long and my tail was so strong
That I really had little to fear.
I was forty feet high, and my cousins and I
Ruled Earth for millions of years.

My four clumsy feet were not very fleet,
So I seldom came up to the shore.
I stayed in the swamp and ate food by the crate.
Now that kind of life I adore!

There's a great deal of lore about the dinosaur,
But we're gone now, and we won't return.
That old refrain about our small brain
Brings me to my other concern.

For I really deplore as I look out my door
What I see you doing these days.
I sorely abhor the way you keep talking of war;
You really should change your ways.

You throw words around, give advice not sound,
Spend money on things that are wrong.
You have a big brain, but it's under a strain,
And you haven't been around very long.

"Don't you know the score?" asked the dinosaur.
"Even my small brain can foresee
That unless you people will learn to agree
You'll soon be extinct, like me."

—Grace Bracker

LESSON PLAN: TRIPS

Purpose

To share personal adventures and discoveries in writing. For most people, past trips (or even imaginary ones) have been highly meaningful times in their lives and recounting them leads to yet further enjoyment. Such accounts provide ready-made narrative material in sequence format replete with sensory details. Travel lends itself to all possible writing forms. The Finlay poem (cited in "resources" below) introduces concrete poetry.

In-class Exercise

Show a variety of travel pictures, both close-ups and distance shots. Magazines, posters, and post cards are good resources. We have used magazines from the Wisconsin Office of Tourism. Ask students to be part of the visual scene in one of the pictures and write about it.

Home Assignment

Instruct the students as follows: Write about a trip in your own life—one you have taken or would like to take. Use the writing form which will best serve your purpose—an article, if you wish to present a tourist review of a place; a story, if there is character interaction and interesting events to focus on; an essay, if there is a personal statement to make about traveling, or a poem, if the trip's essence can be compressed and extracted with feeling.

Resources

Travel and airline magazines, such as *Northwest Magazine Travel/Holiday* and *Vista/USA*.
Ammons, A.R., "Visit" and "Corsons Inlet" (poems)
Didion, Joan, "On Going Home" (essay)
Finlay, Ian Hamilton, "The Horizon of Holland" (poem)
Herman, Michelle, "Blue Ridge Mountains" (journal entry)
Howes, Barbara, "A Letter from the Caribbean" (poem)
Kumin, Maxine, "The Journey" (poem)
Lipsitz, Lou, "Night Train" (poem)
Moses, W.R., "A Trip in a Boat" (poem)

Student Writing

One Giant Step

My darling mother from her nursing home bed
Raised her head, and wishfully said,
"I know I'll leave this earth very soon;
But I do want to stay 'til they get to the moon!"
"I pray you'll be granted your wish," I responded.
Then, excitedly, her reasons she expounded:
"Getting to the moon will make 'can't' obsolete.

After that we'll perform any feat.
We can bring all people of the world together.
We'll probably learn to control the weather.
All earth's starving people we'll feed.
We'll cure disease and blot out need.

War will come into disrepute.
Negotiation will settle every dispute.
Crime can be handled—there is a way,
And we'll be sure on the Moon Walk Day.
Then I can go to my final rest
Knowing, at last, that all here are blessed!''

Mother did not live until Moon Landing Day,
But in my mind I could hear her say,
"Nothing is impossible! Never say can't."
"A leap for mankind" can be more than a chant.

—Leila G. Tubbs

My Trip

When the world is covered
With ice and snow,
The exercise bike is
The way I go.

I jump on the bike
And pick up my book.
I pedal away
And don't even look.

Oh, I've been nowhere.
It wasn't much fun.
But I've biked my four miles
And got the job done.

—Mae Berg

Army Nurse

The year was 1944. I was in the army nurse corps and I was being sent overseas. The third day at sea, we were called to a meeting. The officer in charge told us he was not permitted to reveal our destination for security reasons. However, he said it would be one of three countries and proceeded to describe them. The one that sounded the worst was India. A week later we were called to a second meeting where we learned that our destination was India.

When we crossed the equator, there was a period of celebration. That morning we were ushered below deck and served breakfast in the enlisted men's cafeteria. The breakfast looked very appetizing. However, it had been liberally sprinkled with hot sauce. That afternoon the celebrating continued. We were told to congregate on deck, as everyone had to be initiated into King Neptune's court. Several of the nurses returned to the cabin drenched, and they smelled of rotten eggs. At this point, I decided to hide and felt secure in my upper bunk. Someone must have reported me since two of the ship's crew found me and brought me before King Neptune. King Neptune, a very stout man, was seated on his throne clothed only in a pair of swimming trunks. It seemed that everyone had to kneel and kiss his hairy stomach. They told him I had been found hiding in my cabin. After I kissed his stomach, he said, "In the water with her!" They threw me into a pool of yellow sulphur water where two other crew members dunked me three times. They said everyone else had been dunked once but I was being punished for disobedience. I carried the initiation certificate we received in my wallet for years for fear this would happen again.

—Silver Olsen

A Day in Ireland (excerpt)

County Kerry had much to offer us that day from the extremes of the rugged Macgillycuddy Mountains to the gently rolling hills in the North. We left the Ring of Kerry and traveled along a country road to Limerick. Our driver crept along and we soon discovered the reason. We were sharing the road with quite a number of Holstein cows. Some had a man guiding them but, more often, they were walking and grazing on their own.

We arrived at Limerick late afternoon and discovered, to our delight, that our hotel overlooked the River Shannon. We all wondered if the nonsensical "limerick" originated here. Our guide said it may have started with the Irish Brigade from

Limerick which had been sent to France in the 1600's. The veterans returned with some bawdy barrack-room verses in the limerick metric scheme. But there are other theories.

—Helen M. Campbell

LESSON PLAN: THE SENSES

Purpose

To elicit writing from direct sensory experience. Using the senses brings the writer to his own primary means of experiencing and provides him with something universally human to share. Sensory writing gives practice in memory probing and validates the memory as resource. Descriptive writing introduces the need to choose adjectives carefully and limit them; and it introduces the use of image comparisons, e.g., metaphors and similes.

In-class Exercise

Bring sense-provoking objects and substances to class and pass them around for individual examination. Deal with one sense (only) in a single class meeting. To work with all the senses would require five meetings. Ask the students to list words which come to mind upon smelling, tasting, hearing, touching or seeing these stimulae. Share the resulting word lists by having each read to the group; then ask the students to put their words into sentences or incorporate them into larger units of thought, possibly paragraphs. Again, share orally. Possible objects for class use include: fruit (especially oranges), spearmint, soap, cinnamon, colored tissue or construction paper, shoe polish, bells, fabrics, sandpaper, ice pack (filled), hot water bottle (filled), pictures, ribbons, menthol, toothpaste, ink, and perfume.

Home Assignment

Instruct as follows: from your childhood select a memory which involves the sense of (the particular sense under scrutiny) and try to describe the sensation as though it is being experienced for the first time. Use any writing form you would like—story, poem, essay or article. Paragraphs are also acceptable.

Resources

SMELL	Priestly, J.B., "Waking to the Smell of Bacon," "Making Stew" and "Delight" (essays)
	Kumin, Maxine, "In the Root Cellar" (poem)
	Roethke, Theodore, "Root Cellar" (poem)
	Wallace, Ronald, "Oranges" (poem)
	Williams, William Carlos, "Smell!" (poem)
HEARING	Burr, Gray, "What We Listened For In Music" (poem)
	Dickinson, Emily, "I Heard a Fly Buzz When I Died" and "There Came a Wind Like a Bugle" (poems)
	Poe, Edgar A., "Bells" (poem)
	Rewey, Marion, "In Exchange For Rights to Silence" (poem)
	Kumin, Maxine, "The Hermit Wakes to Bird Sounds" (poem)
	Updike, John, "Sonic Boom" (poem)
	Williams, William Carlos, "The Catholic Bells" (poem)
TASTE	Dickinson, Emily, "I Taste a Liquor Never Brewed" (poem)
	Jong, Erica, "Fruits & Vegetables" (poem)
	Merriam, Eve, "How to Eat a Poem" (poem)
	Stevens, Wallace, "Study of Two Pears" (poem)
	Strand, Mark, "Eating Poetry" (poem)
	Williams, William Carlos, "This Is Just to Say" (poem)
SIGHT	Benchley, Robert, "Looking at Picture Books" (essay)
	Frost, Robert, "Blue-Butterfly Day" (poem)
	Kantor, MacKinlay, "A Man Who Had No Eyes" (story)
	Moffitt, John, "To Look at Any Thing" (poem)
	Pagnucci, Gianfranco, "Adjusting the Eye" (poem)
	Wendt, Viola, "Old Women View the Autumn Leaves" (poem)
	Wilbur, Richard, "Boy At the Window" (poem)
	Williams, William Carlos, "The Red Wheelbarrow" (poem)

TOUCH   Sexton, Anne, "The Touch" (poem)
            Stafford, William, "Traveling Through the Dark"
            (poem)

Student's Writing

The Pebble From Sister Bay

This pearly polished stone
Is elegantly cool to touch
Within my cupping hand.
Aeons of glaciers advancing,
    Receding with patient purpose,
    Then rolling waters pounding.
And the secret of its making
Lies beneath the breaking waves.

—LaVerne Ziegler

Winter Evening

Mamma and I sat on the settee in the large living room of
our farm home. It was a cold, winter evening, so we sat by the
heater where chunks of wood burned with a merry crackle.
The fire glowed red through the square, mica windows. I liked
to put my feet on the fenders, but soon removed them because
they got too hot.

The baby was in bed; I had mamma to myself. In her left
hand, she held a green-covered, open book. Her right hand
rested at the top of the page, ready to flick it over as she finished reading it. I leaned against her, sometimes looking at
her sweet face, crowned by the wavy, auburn hair. Little ten-
drils escaped the hairpins and curled on her neck and pink
cheeks. She smiled with enjoyment as she read *Rebecca of
Sunnybook Farm* to me. When she finished reading, she
called, "Harry, please bring us some of the snow apples from
the barrel in the basement."

My contentment was complete, sitting in the firelight with
my mother, eating a cold, crisp apple, and talking about
Rebecca. The precious world of books had opened to me.

—Edith Pier

The Feel of Dark

I am awakened. It is daylight, but the room is dark. The clock in the adjoining room has struck seven; I faintly hear it ticking. I push back panic, for I can't see.

I toss the bed covers back, one is soft and fluffy, the other has a harder, colder surface. The sheet feels thin and closely woven between my fingers.

I direct myself to the chair on which, last evening, I had draped my clothing. Reaching out, I pass my hands in a slicing motion through the space about me and bump it. Slowly my right, more educated hand, encounters my garments, lifts them from the chair, and places them close to my body. I retreat to the security of my bed, lay my armful next to me as I sit myself on the soft, giving mattress. Running my hand, this time the left one, over the rumpled surface of the bed, I note that the corded, rough feel is that of my slacks. Moving them aside, I grope for the soft, comfortable feel of cotton, the give and take of my elastic stockings.

I slowly dress and rise to leave the bedroom. Feeling for surfaces with my right hand, I encounter the smooth, polished surfaces of the night table, the heavy, glass base of the lamp which I almost overturn in my anxiety to get moving.

After a short spell of insecurity, I approach what should, in my memory, be the door opening. My extended palms are confronted by a flat surface of sameness over which I run my hands, only to find the door closed.

Looking with my hands, I discover the cold, brass of the door knob. I turn it. The door moves to an open position. I push my body forward, slowly and cautiously, my feet moving over a soft, wool layer of carpet into the area ahead. My hands automatically push out to find surfaces on either side of me. I stop. Both hands, palm sides up, peruse the somewhat sand-paperish planes that engulf me, that I mentally recognize as the hall walls. I hesitatingly move forward, my left hand meets the corner of the stair wall and I turn to negotiate the fourteen steps to the living room below. My foot feels its way along the carpet as it goes over the edge of the top step, feelingly finding its way along the plush, cushioned rhythm of equally spaced treads and risers. On the way down, my right hand grasps the square shaped handrail as I hold my breath until I reach the lower floor.

Once more I reach out. I am rewarded by the presence of a chair. Gliding my left hand over the familiar silk-smooth upholstery, I guide my body into it. Mission accomplished, I wait for help.

—Gordon H. Hampel

A Bar of Soap

If I have a clean body, will I have a clean mind when I go to heaven? If I go to hell I won't have a clean mind.

This reminds me of my inclination to take a bath instead of a shower. But at my age I'm fearful of taking a bath. What if I slip in the tub and can't get up? As a matter of fact, I read in the news that Premier Begin slipped in the bath tub and has been in a wheelchair ever since. Maybe that's why he got Israel in trouble with his Golan Heights Law. And Begin is younger than I am. That's why I hesitate to take a bath. Maybe that's why my stories don't smell so good.

—Abe Crane

Brown

Cups of steaming coffee
Warm sand on the beach.
Bark and nuts from a tree
Fresh baked bread within my reach.

Chocolate covered caramels
A field just plowed in spring.
Shiny leather cowboy boots
Brownies, fit for a king.

And the color of his eyes.

—Berdina Padrutt

LESSON PLAN: ON PARENTS AND LOSS

Purpose

To recreate a picture of one's own parents and discover what it was about them that had the most impact on you.

To understand that a mature person does not want to have total possession of one's parents as does a child.

To understand that one's youth and dependent state often distort our image of our parents.

To understand that we are tempted to idealize the lives of the dead.

To understand that a parent's death reminds us that we won't live forever either.

In-class Exercise

Choose one of your parents. Jot down images you suddenly remember about him or her as I call out the sense on which you should focus. You need not use sentences; a phrase or two is fine. Take about two to three minutes for each sense, beginning with the feel and texture images, then smells, sounds, tastes. Then picture him in a certain place, doing a certain activity. Tell the students not to censor memory. Some of the resource poems are about parents who are less than paragons and are still beloved anyway. After listening to lists made by class members, certain topics or thematic ways to organize a piece of writing about a parent should begin to emerge.

Select complementary and not so complementary poems about fathers and mothers from the following list of resource poems.

"The Good Brown Housewife," by Naomi Chase, '54 *Radcliffe Quarterly*
(" . . . how much foolish time
she's spent with brooms,
sweeping out the earth
she'll lie in.")
"The Old Ones," by Mary Tyler, '56 *Radcliffe Quarterly*
("They have forgiven their parents.
Injustice has been wrestled
into the grave . . . ")
"My Mother Said," by Mary Carlton Swope, '59 *Radcliffe Quarterly*
(. . . "& all the while
she was on the telephone
running things she didn't
want to run. Don't waste yourself

You only have one life
my mother said'')
"Parents," by William Meredith, *The New Yorker*
("What it must be like to be an angel
or a squirrel, we can imagine sooner . . .")
"Waving," by Dave Smith, *The New Yorker*
(Watching his own children, a man recalls his father:
"he is still there, waving,
and I am waving, beating
the air with my arms,
bruised and afraid,")
"My Mother's Feet," by Stanley Plumly, *Poetry Magazine*
(. . . "How no shoe fit them,
and how she used to prop them,
having dressed for bed,
letting the fire in the coal-stove blue")
"My Mother's Lips," by C.K. Williams, *The New Yorker*
(. . . "My mother, all through my childhood
when I was saying something to her, something important,
would move her lips as I was speaking
so that she seemed to be saying, under her breath, the very
words I was saying as I was saying them.")
"The Kiss," by Robert Pack, *Poetry Magazine*
(A father walks out in spring with his son and his kite
to check apple trees. He is seized with love
for his child and spontaneously enacts some
dramatic play that delights them both.)
"Tide Pools," by Dave Smith, *Poetry Magazine*
(Here again a father initiates some dramatic play
with his family at the beach before they drive home:
"The road home will be long and dark, the stars cold,
but collected, like this, we will be buoyed beyond
the dark snags and splinters of what we once were.")
"Tortures," by Stephen Dunn in his book *Circus of Needs*
(In telling a child about war tortures a father seems to
enjoy torturing his own sensitive son with lurid tales.)
"The Horsewoman," by Maxine Kumin in her book *House Bridge
Fountain Gate*
(A young girl turns herself inside out to impress
her alcoholic father who "kept his indifferent
eyes away/ from his wishbone of a daughter.")

Home Writing Assignment

The following writing ideas should jostle memories of experiences already remembered through the in-class exercise and conversation following it. Select one of the following eight writing ideas each week for a writing session which has a thematic focus. Poem, short story, or personal essay may be used.

1. Tell about a time of intense hero worship for a parent.
2. Tell about a time when a parent somehow disappointed you. Was he too controlling, did he ignore you, did he exert unfair pressure for you to conform, was he too timid, too pessimistic?
3. Show a picture of him when he is really at his best. Try to say why you are indebted to him.
4. Tell about something you have learned or failed to learn from your parents which has influenced your own parenting.
5. Describe some object or activity which always serves to remind you of a parent long since dead.
6. Tell about a time when you felt valuable and worthwhile because your parent(s) took the time to play some sort of imaginative game, or sing, or tell you stories or read to you. Go into detail about what the game, song, book was, and why the experience was so memorable.
7. Tell about a time you remember functioning best as a parent with your own children, respecting them and bracketing your own needs in order to help them to grow to independence.
8. Tell about a time you had a stunningly clear awareness that you won't always be here on this earth either.

Cemeteries

Meadowbrook

Upon the hill
Your graves
Look out
Across the meadow
And the brook
To where you lived
So many years
Nurtured us

With food and thought
With love and discipline
Sent us forth
With hope and pride
Then passed beyond the pall
Before you knew
How well you shaped us
To our destinies

—Benjamin Brothers

My Tapestry

My guardian angel, I believe,
the moment I was born,
handed me some weaving warp,
and many balls of yarn.
There was yarn of every color,
dark and light shades too,
and the angel whispered softly:
"When your life is through,
your tapestry will be finished.
I pray it's a lovely creation.
Whoever helps to shape your life
here will weave his donation."
I've studied my tapestry closely,
I see many gold threads all through.
I know they were woven by Mother,
my guide for whatever I do.

—Leila Tubbs

My Mud Mania

Believe it or not, there is an art to making mud cakes. I learned that art very young, as mud and imagination were about the only toys I possessed as a child.

I assume I took to making mud cakes as a means of mimicking my mother, who always had her hands in dough of some sort. Those were the days before baker's bread, and with a family of nine to feed, flour was always on Mother's apron. Flour came in 50 pound cloth bags. The name brands were stamped on in bold colors. The white sacks were an added benefit and Mother had an ample supply. From flour sacks she sewed dish towels and underwear.

My underwear was not mini-bras and panties, but bloomers and middies. After cutting a pattern on newspaper, my mother fashioned my lingerie from flour sacks. My bloomers had names such as Eco, Gold Medal, Kitchen-Tested Flour, Best Triple XXX, and Robin Hood. The vest-like middies also had names on them. Sometimes I wore an Eco vest with a King Midas bloomer. I was very careful not to bend from the waist for fear I might reveal my name-brand underwear.

On Sundays, undies were put in a copper boiler on the back of the wood-burning kitchen stove to steep in soft water and home-made soap. The bold names gradually succumbed to the strong, hot solution and they bleached white as snow.

In this "get up" I would stand and watch Mother stooped over a large dishpan of light, springy dough, punching and kneading. It looked like so much fun I was eager to try it too. Because my mother was very conservative and very clean, her ears were deaf to my insistent begging. She would never surrender even a smidgen from the mountain of her precious mixture. To satisfy my itching fingers, I grudgingly escaped to the creek below our house to engage in my own mud cuisine.

From the dump I salvaged sardine cans, broken dishes or any type of container that held the prospect of an interesting mold. Like a packrat I hoarded up a good supply of utensils against the trunk of an old oak tree that stretched out over the shallow creek bed.

I mixed my ingredients in a small tin pail that once contained "Plow Boy," my father's favorite tobacco. After filling the pail half full of clean damp soil dug from the bank, I used the thin end of a slender piece of shingle to stir in one full "pork and bean" can of creek water. I had it down to a science. This exact amount gave the mixture a pliable texture that did not stick all over my hands.

That shingle also proved to be an excellent spatula. On an old board, I would pat out loaves of bread in miniature. A clap on all four sides of the mud with the shingle made a perfect rectangular loaf. An added dollop of mud gave an instant raise of a mounded top.

To make corn bread meant a trip to the "grocery" crib for an ear of corn. I can still feel my tender fingers shelling the hard, glassy kernels, exposing the red furry cob. I would pick the kernels off row by row. One big ear filled a tin can full. These yellow grains provided an interesting texture and added color. Father had oats in the granary—why not oatmeal? These mixtures, pressed in the oval sardine cans, turned out molds I had not seen the likes of even on Mother's table.

For special occasions, a cautious trip to the chicken house added an egg or two. Cow salt was always on hand upstairs in the barn, and heaped up in mounds on mud cakes, was frosting or even ice cream right in the middle of July!

My imagination took me to the orchard for green apples. Chopped and mixed with mud, they were mouth-watering. Plums and cherries between mud crust were blue-ribbon winners. Cookies decorated with cherry pits and weed seeds were lined up by the dozens. I made doughnuts by rolling long slender ropes from mud and pinching the ends together.

From my outdoor bakery, I unconsciously observed the business of nature. Barefoot in the creek water, I saw the polliwogs in all stages of maturity. Occasionally a green frog swam underneath the overhanging sod. Dragonflies and water skeeters skimmed the surface, schools of minnows played in the deeper pools, sparrows bathed among the pebbles, and one time an ugly crayfish caused me to flee to the house. A small grass snake frightened me into moving my entire bakery upstream by the old plank bridge. I became aware of the magnificence of the sky, for I had been warned it was dangerous to be by the creek and that I should return to the house if a storm threatened. I had heard dragonflies would sew your eyes shut, and that if a turtle got hold of your big toe, it would not let go until it thundered. I believe my older sisters told me these old wives' tales when I was very small to make their task of keeping me away from the creek easier. Although I did not quite believe them, these predictions nagged at the back of my mind.

If I left them in the sun, my concoctions baked hard as bullets. They lasted indefinitely if I handled them carefully. Even though no-one snitched my goodies, they sometimes met with disaster. Wandering chickens would pick out my crunchy, nutty fillings of corn and oats. The ever-present ants thought it was a picnic.

Rain insisted upon reshaping my sculptures into grotesque blobs. Even the wind had a way of dusting up my salt icings. I was highly insulted one morning to find that a cow had left the essence of grass splattered in my bakery. I soon learned such precious items had to be protected.

In the corner of the corn crib I put together a play house. Wooden peach boxes stacked up in cupboard fashion displayed my culinary delights. Dried weed seeds from yellow dock looked exactly like coffee grounds. My Norwegian descent prompted me to stock my shelves with cans and cans of it. My prized possession, because of its reality, was an old leaky coffee pot, cover intact. I made it good as new by pulling a piece of cloth through the hole in the bottom. On an empty five-gallon paint pail turned upside down, with water from the creek, I brewed myself a pot of yellow dock coffee. Like a gourmet I sat down to eat and drink with my imaginary company, urging them to try each of my delicacies.

Summer gave way to fall, and returning home from school one afternoon, I found the crib filled with ear corn. The contents of my play house were in a heap outside the door. Viewing the conglomeration, I understood the corn was the rightful tenant; but from the mess I did manage to save the coffee pot by sticking it in a deep crevice in the old stone wall. Losing my play house did not matter much to me, for the days were growing cold and the long walk home from the country schoolhouse drained my energies. Indoors and the warmth of the stove were more inviting. Next summer, I told myself, I would make a better bakery, anyway.

But I do not remember engaging so diligently in my mud mania again. It was a passing phase of my childhood, an experience I remember with a smile. I forgive you, Mother, for not surrendering your dough. I realize how hard you worked to turn mountains of flour into crusty home-made bread. I have not been able to equal a single loaf. Thank you for the middies and bloomers you sewed with loving hands. A rare privilege it was to sit unsupervised in the quiet of the country, observing nature, exercising my imagination and my hands. Mud beneath my fingernails, freckled and barefooted, sitting in my flour sack bloomers among my mud creations, I must have been a sight to behold. The greatest bonus of it all was, the fun was free—and so was I.

—Beulah Uren

Sweeter Than Sugar

Pa never did like sugar lumps. He never liked to stir sugar around in his coffee to sweeten it either. He did have a "little sugar habit" of his own, though. When Pa had almost finished his coffee, he would put a whole teaspoonful of sugar in his mouth and let it slowly dissolve between the final sips.

Ma often apologized for Pa by saying he acquired the habit in Norway. She said they seldom had cake or cookies there, so for something sweet at the end of a meal, they drank their coffee with a little sugar. As I recall, though, Ma daintily lifted a sweet teaspoonful herself sometimes—when she and Pa sat alone together drinking their afternoon coffee.

Pa drank only three cups of coffee a day. The first he savored early in the morning as soon as he got the fire in the old kitchen stove hot enough to brew a potful. From my bed above the kitchen, I could hear Pa lifting the lid from the cookstove, poking around in the firebox, crumpling papers and laying pieces of kindling ready to burn. It was my job to see that the basket by the stove was filled with kindling. I would gather up chips and bits of bark from the woodpile, twigs and dry sticks from beneath the trees, and corncobs scattered below the pig pen.

When I heard Pa so busy downstairs, I was glad I hadn't forgotten to fill the kindling basket. The stovepipe went up through my bedroom, and soon sparks were popping and tapping inside the long black cylinder. I heard the pouring of water, and the crunch of coffee beans told me Pa was turning the iron crank round and round on the coffee grinder.

Then I knew it wouldn't be long before the smell of coffee would be floating upstairs. The aroma was Ma's cue to get up, and I heard her go quietly down the squeaky stairs. As the finger of dawn stretched along the horizon, birds chirped in the cedars below the house. The dog waiting on the porch by the screen door gave a soft bark to tell Pa to "get a move on." He was anxious to fetch the cows from the night pasture. The sound of roosters crowing from within the hen house came through the open window. An outcast answered from his perch in the pig house. They always had some kind of contest going, but I never understood the rules nor who won.

Gradually, I'd drift back to sleep to the clinking of coffee cups, and the muffled voices of Ma and Pa downstairs. I wondered what they found to talk about so early in the morning.

Pa sat down for his second cup of the day at breakfast. He had already milked the cows and hauled the milk to the cheese factory. I would stand by Pa in the milk rig with one arm around his long leg to balance myself as the wagon bumped down the rough dirt road. Sometimes he even let me hold the reins. After emptying the milk cans, Pa visited with the other farmers for a while, and then returned home. Pa was pretty hungry and thirsty by this time. As we ate breakfast, he told Ma the latest news.

Pa's third cupful of coffee, without fail, was enjoyed mid-afternoon. Ma always had the green and yellow enamel pot steeping on the back of the black stove. When she heard Pa coming for his three o'clock cup, she would go to the pantry for a fried cake or a white rolled sugar cookie with a raisin stuck in the middle. Pa would sit down by the round oak table, cross his long legs and indulge. He often lamented to Ma about the "too hot" coffee—to no avail. Impatient with its cooling process, he would pour a little in the saucer and skillfully lift it to his mouth. Cautiously, he drew the hot brew between his lips. It was a long time before I learned the real purpose of a saucer.

When Pa was working in the field, his coffee came to him. In an empty sorghum pail, Ma would pack a jar of hot coffee, a couple of those everlasting fried cakes wrapped in wax paper salvaged from an empty box of corn flakes, a container of sugar, and a teaspoon. As she slipped the pail into my hand, the inevitable words, "don't lose the teaspoon," fell on my ears. I knew Ma didn't have any extra teaspoons to lose.

With responsibility heavy on my shoulders, I hurried through the garden gate, across the plank bridge, and into the meadow where I followed the cow trail. Dandelions peeked from behind fence posts. Pa called them "Ma's flowers" because she poured water on those which grew by the pump stand. A gold finch sat on the purple blossoms of the bull thistles, and the burrs on the burdock were green and prickly. Ma said they were "Pa's flowers" because the burrs hitched rides on his overalls.

Killdeer with their long, skinny legs zig-zagged and flopped around ahead of me. I was onto their broken wing act—and besides, I would never touch their nest of speckled eggs hidden in the long grass growing in a dark green circle around a pie of dried cow dung.

The steep hill up through the poplar grove offered no challenge. The silver dollar leaves quivered overhead. I stopped to look at a certain tree where my older sister had carved a heart in the trunk. Inside the heart were the initials A.R. and K.C. Secretly, I thought I would do the same someday.

From the top of the hill I could see my Pa sitting erect on the high metal seat of the binder, guiding his big black team along the cut edge of the yellow grain field. The horses arched their thick necks and leaned into the heavy collars as they lifted their muscular legs in unison, sharing their burden. The burnished wooden reel turned slowly round and round to the rhythmic clicking of the sickle as it mowed the straws, leaving a stubble path behind.

Bundles of oats lay scattered in the shaggy field, and bobbing red-winged blackbirds gleaned the kernels lost in the disturbance. As Pa waved at me, I thought I was looking at a colored picture I had seen on the cover of a farm magazine. I let myself fly down the hill so Pa and I would reach the end of the field at the same time. Pa's face showed he was happy to see me, and he said some kind words in Norwegian about how "snill" I was to bring him his lunch.

Stepping back down off the binder, he pulled his big red handkerchief from his back pocket and wiped his face to rid it of dust and sweat. The horses relaxed into a hipshot stance, chewed their bits and dropped their heads. Pa tossed a couple of oat bundles together, and we sat down on them side by side. Putting his cap beside him and prying the lid from the tin pail with his pocket knife, he was ready for lunch. We shared his fried cakes, occasionally a sip of coffee, and talked about the horses. It was a hot day for them, and they would need their shoulders washed down with salt water tonight to toughen their hides against collar sores.

Scanning the skies, we hoped we would get all the oats out and shocked before rain fell. He said the grain was standing well, and the kernels were plump and heavy. There would be many shocks to set up on this field. We hoped we wouldn't run out of twine before quitting time, and that the binder canvas would hold out until the harvest was done.

We noticed the wild grape vines crawling on the fence, the nuts hanging on the hickory trees, the wild raspberry bushes and the sumac, already showing signs of flaming.

Sitting by Pa, I saw how his big brown calloused hands always had a bruise or scratch on them, and his worn, oily shoes creased to the contours of his feet. The shoe laces criss-crossed the tongue and went through little eyelets that sparkled in the sun. The laces ended in a double knot with frayed ends.

By this time, Pa was ready for his grains of sugar. After giving me a taste, he put the remainder in his mouth, and I heard the spoon clink into the pail.

While Pa finished his coffee, I rubbed the horses velvety noses and lifted the foretops from their sweaty heads. As Pa pressed the cover back on the pail and situated his cap on his head again, he said I should start the cows home. Soon he was turning the horses to cut another swatch, and I was swinging the pail on my way home. Leisurely, I followed the cows back beyond the hill where I could see my home. Smoke curled from the chimney and Ma was stooped over in the garden. My hayrope swing hung limp from the arm of a big oak tree. White chickens were picking and scratching in the barnyard and the big woodpile stared at me, reminding me the woodbox was almost empty. I left the cows in the meadow to graze until milking time, and ran to the house with the lunch pail—spoon and all.

Pa and I picnicked in the sunshine of spring among the plowed furrows of black dirt. We shared summer lunches on windrows of new mown hay, when the air was heavy with the scent of wilt. And in autumn we rested our backs against the musky shocks of corn fodder, and heard south-bound wild geese toss talk in the skies. These memories are sweeter than the teaspoons of sugar we shared along the fencerow.

—Beulah Uren

Nothing

Mom was mad at me. It was the day I came home late for lunch with my pants torn and my shoes muddy. A couple of us guys spent the morning up at the Pine Stump Hole fishing. Fish didn't bite so we horsed around. That's how I got my shoes muddy and my pants torn.

Mom didn't talk to me while I was eating but afterward she said "George, you WILL stay in the yard this afternoon! You WILL have to learn to be prompt and neat!"

The guys and I had been planning on swimming down at the dam that afternoon, but as Mom had her dander up, I didn't mention it. I just said "O.K. Mom," and went outside to sit on the lawn bench. I wondered why Mom, and Dad too, always came down so hard on me. I most always do my chores. I don't cause trouble in school. I'm not mean to my little brother. I don't sass my parents or other grown ups. Those pants are sorta old, and those shoes can be cleaned. I didn't mind eating cold meat and potatoes. She didn't need to get mad at me!

As I was sitting there I saw a wren fly into the bird house. It had a worm in its beak! That meant the eggs were hatched! The babies were here! I watched that busy little bird make twenty-two trips to the bird house. Each time it came with a kinda squashed-up worm. Then the wren stayed away for a while so I watched the clouds. I do that lotsa times. Some look like dogs, some like horses, others lions, pigs, sheep, mountains, cotton candy, wild geese—lotsa things. Today I saw one that looked like a fat lady, running.

While watching the clouds I heard something, so I closed my eyes to listen. I hear better that way. Then I heard a lot of things. A cow bellering, a dog barking, Kazkowski's lawn mower, a car that wouldn't start, some guy yelling and a mourning dove that called twenty-two times. Heard our TV too. Mom must have finished all the kitchen work and was watching her soap show.

I got up from the bench to get a drink of water from the garden hose. When I first turned on the water it was hot and rubbery so I let it run for a long time. Then I spotted our mean old tomcat snoozing. I caught him good. He just flew when the cold water hit him. I had a long cold drink and went back to the lawn bench. I took out my knife and sat there for a while whittling on a willow stick, just making long, thin curled shavings. When my stick was used up I played that knife game, baseball. It's sorta like mumbly peg. I played twelve games, nine innings each.

I heard water running in the kitchen. Golly! It was late afternoon! Mom was starting to make supper. She looked out the window, saw me sitting there, came outside and asked what I had been doing.

As I was right there all afternoon, I said, "Nothing." She got kinda mad at me again.

—George Hartman

Roots and Rememberings

Today, I strolled through the yard by my usual route to speak encouragement to the plants and flowers along the way. I came to the pansy bed where the blossoms nodded brightly at me in the sun. My father was stooped over, pulling grass and weeds, while a windmill creaked and groaned behind him. He straightened and said, "This triangle always was a nuisance to mow; it's easier just to pull the weeds out of the pansies. Look at that; it's one of my favorites." He pointed to one with rich, purple tones. "And don't you like the yellow one with the dark markings?"

I agreed and thought to myself that a farmer growing pansies in his spare time was a bit of an enigma. Now that I think of it, though, after shipping thousands of cattle and hogs to market for profit, it must have been a nice change to grow something just for the joy and beauty of it.

My father faded along with the windmill, so I headed to the flower garden by the big rock in the front yard. Grandma Buckner was bent over the bleeding hearts, a stem of vivid red hearts outlined against her thin, calloused hand.

"Uncommonly pretty this year, ain't they? And come see the roses. I have a new salmon color I like especially; I'll bring the scissors so we can snip a bouquet for you to take home. We'll mix them with those white ones." Grandma slapped along in her faded carpet slippers; I noticed she had, as usual, cut out the sides to ease the pressure on her painful bunions. When Grandma disappeared in search of the roses, I turned to the iris bed.

Miss Kirk stood there with her ramrod posture, prim mouth, and pointed nose. "You should have some of these Japanese species for your garden. They contrast nicely with the common varieties and are a lovely deep purple." Her English was as precise and correct as when she conducted her literature classes, but she was attired in garden hat and gloves, and her shoes were actually a little bit dirty. She went in search of a spade and bucket and did not return, so I walked on.

I stopped by the butternut tree in the back yard. Grandpa Buckner stood there, hands clasped behind his back, looking at it with a speculative eye. "Butternut works mighty good for whittling. You ought to have a bench here. Be a good place to set in the breeze and whittle a chain."

"I know, Grandpa. If I get a chair and a butternut board, will you whittle a chain?"

He grinned and nodded. I turned to get them; but when I glanced back, only the butternut leaves waved in the breeze.

I walked slowly toward the strawberry bed. Grandpa Mefford was hoeing steadily, but straightened as I approached and leaned on his hoe. He wore his faded blue overalls, a wide-brimmed straw hat, and high topped work shoes which turned up at the toes like those of an elf. "Strawberries are a heap of work, but they taste mighty good when a feller's hungry." He brushed his full, white moustache with the back of his hand. "Your grandma just baked some shortcake this morning. Go tell her I said you should see if it's fit to eat." He grinned mischievously. His grin faded and only a butterfly hovered over the strawberries.

I turned to see Grandma Mefford standing by a bed of fluttering, nodding nasturtiums. She smiled and gestured toward the mass of bloom. "Showy, aren't they? I planted Golden Gleam and Jewel Mixed this year. I always was partial to nasturtiums." She smoothed her apron carefully. "We ought not to stand here in the hot sun; I came out without a sunbonnet. Come in. I just took some shortcake out of the oven, and there's a bowl full of strawberries." We turned to go, but she melted into air; I walked thoughtfully toward the house.

The sudden ringing of the telephone startled me, and I ran up the steps.

My mother's cheerful voice came over the wire. "Hello. What are you up to this Sunday afternoon?"

"Just strolling around looking at the flowers and garden."

"You should see my flowering crab. Just loaded with blossoms and so are half a dozen others on this street. They're at their peak now."

"Wish I could see them," I murmured. "How are your strawberries?"

"Oh, they look promising. You should come and help me eat them in about three weeks."

My mother chatted amiably on. I held tightly to the phone, soaking in the familiar, hearty tones of her voice, so that I could recall them when she said her final goodby.

—Dottie Kermicle

LESSON PLAN: PROSE POEMS

Purpose

To understand that prose poems can be embedded in other forms, even their own essays.

To understand that what a person says and how he says it unerringly reveals character.

To understand that commonplace, even ugly, images can be used powerfully and become beautiful.

To understand the power of paradox in "temporary" and "timeless."

To understand the device of inserting what characters may be imagining in their heads to reveal character ("he gazes fondly . . . " "I imagine my lawn torn up").

To understand that we are mortal, that we are outlasted by nature and by art.

In-class Exercise

List five or six routine chores you perform daily. Choose one and describe that ordinary process or task in a glorified, pompous way, making it seem far more unique and important than it in fact is, making you, the executor of the act seem far more indispensable than you in fact are.

Home Assignment

Choose another one of the tasks, or continue on with the one you warmed up on in class. Try to choose words that will elevate the task to the heroic. You can try to make the task or process stand for some universal process if you can pull it off.

Resources to Illustrate Writing Idea

1. Excerpt from essay on "Plumbing" by John Updike, beginning "Eventually see, it leaks" and ending "All around us, we are outlasted."
2. Prose poems by Vern Rutsala, Robert Bly, Ron Wallace, and Richard Shelton.
3. *Seven Lake Superior Poets,* anthology, Bear Cult Press, Box 468, Ashland, Wisconsin 54806.

Afternoon Concert

There was excitement in the falling rain that afternoon at Grandma's house. Not only could I see it as it pelted out of the clouds, but I heard its rhythms immediately as it began to spatter onto the roof over my bedroom. Slowly at first, like experimental fingers, it tapped gently at my window, but with accelerating speed the drops misted off the glass onto the slanting overhang. The tin-roof tympani had begun in earnest. As the drumming increased its intensity, the rain bounced off the gutters, each drop throbbing a metallic melody. The staccato accents came in repeated waves as the sheets of rain were blown against the house and wind-swept into spray.

With the thunder booming through the background of rain music, I snuggled into Gram's feather bed, minding not at all that I was shut in by the storm. I liked the earfilling downpour on the receptive roof which was now being cleansed of the summer dust.

Soon the rain would spurt and gurgle down into the rattling cistern after Grandma switched the lever on the downspout—and we would have plenty of water again.

—Mary Brodzeller
Courtesy of *Heartland Journal*

Examples of writing ideas gleaned from poems:

1. Read Erika Mumford's poem "Pierre Loti Visits the Maharaja of Travancore" (*Poetry,* February 1984) especially the last lines:

Monkeys
skipped before him. The sun beat down.
Beyond the palace crashed the desolate sea.
And nothing reminded him of home.

Tell about a time you were far from home and it was so exotic
and foreign, nothing reminded you of home.

2. Describe a time when your happiness depended on being able,
   "to bear some bearable deprivation" or defeat.

3. Be "There, where you never were," and imagine all the sensual details of it.

4. Describe a person who really "got the face he deserves,"
   whose character, for good or for worse, has surfaced in his
   face.

5. Describe a beloved child in a queer, unsentimental way.

6. Take a person with the slimmest of lives and dignify it with a
   history, a "rush of anecdote and regret."

7. Take off on this idea: man is an animal that has to find something to do with his hands.

8. Describe a time when someone gave you a blank check—describe what you did, what it meant then. You may use the idea
   of a blank check metaphorically if you want to.

9. Describe a time when someone gave you a script or a prescrip-
   tion of how to act, not a blank check. How did you react?

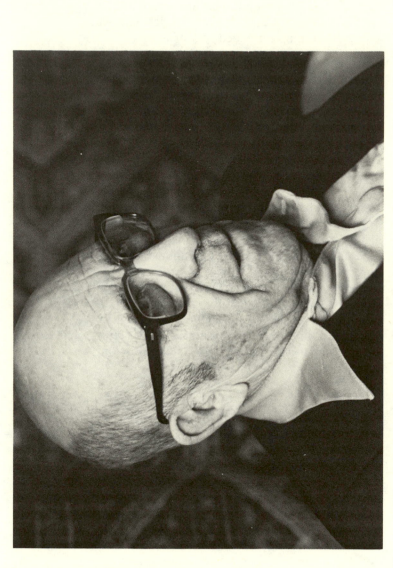

Benjamin Brothers began writing poetry for his senior center writing class friends but is now an active member of his state fellowship of poets. Photo by Brent Nicastro.

Chapter 8

Touchstones of Validity:
The Teachers' Rewards

The Ravens

You glide above the canyon's yawning maw
Black wings outstretched,
You catch the upward thrust of thermals
Rising from the giant gash in earth's rocky crust.
You dip close to my reclining form on the canyon's rim,
To where I lie on the rocks, heat soaking into my bones,
A shaggy juniper shielding me from burning rays,
Then you rise again in graceful arc,
Seeming to say:
"This is the real me!
I am not the carrion eater in the road
Pecking at pitiful pieces of flesh,
Nor am I the dreary perpetual croaker of 'Nevermore.'
I am a creature of beauty and joy.
I am borne by an unseen force
Above the mundane limits of earth.
From here I can view my universe
And watch the sun cast its shadows on the rocks
Changing them to brilliant reds and ochres,
Back again to russets and dull browns."

Oh ravens,
I envy you your faith in those powers you do not
    understand.
I admire the loveliness of pattern in your flight.
I am grateful for the sight of you,
Riding the thermals
Above the canyon.

—From "On the Rim of the Canyon,"
Grace Bracker

One way to assess the rewards a task brings is to look at the challenges it presents. Our challenges, always keen, have increased with time. When we began teaching, we worked hard to put together enough plans and activities to provide for an entire course. There would come a time, we hoped, when enough resources would be assembled to complete a "package" we could use repeatedly with each new session. Surely the pupils would acquire the basics in a matter of weeks—two or three sessions, perhaps—and go off on their own to write. Then we could start over with our assembled bag of tricks. But after a few sessions we realized there were people in our classes who had come to stay. Whether they'd learned the basics or not, they had no intention of "graduating" and settling down on their own to write. They needed the group and planned to remain with it indefinitely. At the same time, new students were continually entering. Beyond the program's initial classes, we have rarely enrolled a 'batch' of all-new students. We have had 'new' and 'old' simultaneously. Because of this mixture of repeating and inexperienced participants we have had to keep increasing the repertoire of activities to avoid repetition. Always mindful that the writing program exists for the students and must suit their needs, we have had to develop assignments which will challenge many levels of expertise.

Hens

The woman throws fresh straw
on the floor of the henhouse.
Ah, the delight, the hearty conversation
among the hens.
In joyful release from boredom
they scratch and duck
and tell each other
how springy this straw,
how deep, how clean.
They hope some sweet grains
have been missed by the combine.
Vigorously, they aim to find out.

Now and again
with staccato clucks they run to the woman
and peck at her shoes
in gratitude.

—Viola Wendt

In old age, things become more intense rather than less so. Things get more poignant—so many associations—everything reverberating with everything else.

—John Hall Wheelock

* * *

Just as writing is personal and individualized, so is teaching. The writing teacher is working with individuals who participate actively in their own training process. Such teaching is learner-oriented as opposed to subject-oriented. It must be dynamic and organic. It won't let the teacher merely "be," won't allow "canned" presentations. It pushes, pulls, teases, and trips and it requires new beginnings, further variations. Flexibility is essential. The teacher must dream up new methods to meet new needs. Indeed, getting varied individuals to write is a challenge. Getting them to improve their writing over time is yet a further challenge.

For the beginning writer, the thrill of getting something down on paper for the first time is so exhilarating that the product is almost sacred. Tampering with that product is scary because the accomplishment might get undone. It might never happen again. The teacher must serve as a trustworthy guide or a coach, if the student is to be led through the necessary stages of production, revision, and refinement. There must be faith that the process will pay off. Consider the rewards of a writer-turned-teacher who is able to do all of this. It may not happen immediately, of course, but eventually. For the successful teacher, the advent of each new session brings the anticipation of a new configuration of individuals to work with: new problems, new projects, new styles—the chance for new learning. The teacher who is equally excited to be a learner, the one who seeks mastery yet knows it will always be elusive, is the sort who enjoys teaching older adults to write. The rewards for such a teacher lie in the effort itself nearly as much as in the tangible outcomes.

There are other rewards, public as well as private. Recognition in the community is very satisfying. Running into an appreciative student at a shopping center can kindle new awe in the eyes of a friend or family member who may be accompanying you. The student stops to say how you, the teacher, have changed her life, given her new purpose. And more formal occasions bring more formal rewards. Our program has sponsored conferences, public readings, and publications which provide leadership and acclaim for staff members. We find our program and our names in the newspapers often. Other professional writers coming into contact with the program by participating on a panel, judging a contest, doing a reading or leading a workshop, have been amazed at the students' knowledge and skill. They give warm strokes to the teachers. Of course, any student's achievement in publication or public reading reflects favorably on the teacher.

* * *

Art can be a vital tool in one's life. You don't have to conceive of art in Olympian terms to see how it helps people to learn to think for themselves, to sharpen their own perceptual capacities and heighten their sense of self, while at the same time allowing an immediate sense of other people's unique subjective experience. Art thus has an important role to play in staving off the standardization of society.

—Knud Jensen

* * *

The richest rewards are more private. They are rooted in communications and the ongoing learning process. They happen when a learner feels accepted and comes to understand. To be understood is joyously confirming. When you, the teacher, are understood, you know your efforts have paid off. Then, if the student takes that bit of understanding and goes further, builds on it, brings his own interpretation to it and branches out in some new way, teaching becomes all the more exciting. Conversely, the teacher of a small group has the chance to be a listener, an active listener, who is working at understanding the questions, concerns and insights of her students. The students, too, feel confirmed by this; it is an extraordinary way to teach and brings full circle the abundant rewards of authentic communication. It leads to empathy, that pinnacle of human understanding.

With experience, the teacher comes to a curious paradox regarding the nature of involvement with students. The relationship is one of friendship, in a sense, and the teacher is mindful of an equal status vis à vis maturity and autonomy; yet she is responsible for the learning of these "friends" in a particular area—writing—and must create the distance which can allow her to remain a critic and an authority. On the one hand, she may be charmed by them as individuals; on the other, she must assess their skills objectively and let them know where they stand as writers. She is involved, yet she is detached. This sensitive relationship requires a caring stance aligned with professional credibility. Being both kind and honest is not always easy. Success in such a delicate balance is infinitely rewarding.

* * *

Influence creates nothing: it awakens. The power of an influence comes from the fact that it has only revealed to me some part of myself that was still unknown to me.

—*Andre Gide*

* * *

The writer who teaches learns more about writing. Some of this new learning comes about indirectly through preparation for class activities—setting goals, researching, collecting resources, and critiquing manuscripts. Some comes during class exchanges—discussion of writing concerns and experiences. Often, after such talk, the teacher feels inspired in some aspect of her own writing; she may come to a new topic or theme, or she may see a new direction for an old one. Of course, student material, whether shared orally or in writing, belongs to the student and must not be usurped by the teacher. Instead the responsible teacher points out its possibilities and, if needed, helps the student achieve his own writing goals. But if she is willing to submit one of her own manuscripts now and then for critiquing by the class, she may receive directly some useful suggestions for its improvement. One teacher supplied each of her students with a photocopy of one of her children's stories for analysis at home and received several helpful suggestions for refining it. The experience was mutually satisfactory. Learning, moreover, is not strictly writing-related. Exposure to a small group, especially in the context of the intimacy shared by writers, abounds with personal anecdotes and philosophies. One learns about people.

What about doing all of this with students over sixty? That's the best part. It is a privilege to be among people who, unlike the general population, believe that the advantages of aging outweigh the disadvantages; people who have come to an air of transcendence which accepts the reality of physical decline without being devastated by it; people who believe that old age brings the fullest strength of character and independence of thought. Older people who are serious about writing have more to give than any other age group. They have accumulated all of the basic human experiences and understandings and have begun to ponder them. For most it is a time of celebrating longevity, and rejoicing each in the singular identity that it has brought. For older writers, writing is the heady culmination—the means to sum up and leave something of themselves behind. They see the writing teacher as a benefactor who makes this possible. Their gratitude is especially heightened because they are so ready for writing; writing is uniquely appropriate for their evolved stage in the life span. A teacher can only thrive on such receptivity, such appreciation.

Booklist: Resources for Teacher and Classroom Use

FOR THE TEACHER'S READING

Three Genres, Stephen Minot, Prentice Hall
An Introduction to Haiku, Harold G. Henderson, Doubleday Anchor
Writing with Power, Peter Elbow, Oxford University Press
Reading Modern Poetry, Engle and Carrier, Scott, Foresman and Co.
An Introduction to Poetry, X. J. Kennedy, Little, Brown, and Co.
poetry handbook, babette deutsch, Universal Library, Grosset and Dunlap
The Elements of Style, Strunk & White, Macmillan
How to Write Better, reprint from *The Christian Science Monitor*
Writer's Market, Writer's Digest Books
Write the Story of Your Life, Ruth Kavin, Hawthorn/Dutton
Writing the Natural Way, Gabrielle Rico, J. B. Tarcher, Inc.
The Triggering Town, Richard Hugo, W. W. Norton & Co.
To Make a Prairie, Maxine Kumin, University of Michigan Press
Journey Toward Poetry, Jean Burden, October House, Inc.
Writing the Australian Crawl, William Stafford, University of Michigan Press
Tips for Article Writers, Jerry Apps, Wisconsin Regional Writers, 215 Oak Hill, Green Bay, WI 54301
The Gates of Excellence, Katherine Paterson, Elsevier/Nelson
One Writer's Beginnings, Eudora Welty, Harvard University Press
Becoming a Writer, Dorothea Brande, J. B. Tarcher, Inc.
The New Diary, Tristine Rainer, J. B. Tarcher, Inc.
Letters to a Young Poet, Rainer Maria Rilke, W. W. Norton & Co.
Writing Fiction, Arturo Vivante, Writer
Thirty Ways to Help You Write, Fran Weber Shaw, Bantam Books, Inc.
Rose, Where Did You Get That Red, Kenneth Koch, Vintage

TO SHARE WITH STUDENTS

The Second Tree from the Corner, E. B. White, Harper & Bros.
The Joy and Adventure of Growing Younger, Mary Kimbrough,
   Concordia Publishing House, St. Louis
Selected Poems of Ai Qing, University of Indiana Press
Reflections on a Gift of Watermelon Pickle, anthology, Lothrop,
   Lee, and Shepard
The Essay: Subjects and Stances, Edward Corbett, Prentice-Hall
The Voice That Is Great Within Us, anthology, Bantam Poetry
Poet's Choice, anthologies, Delta Books
You Keep Waiting for Geese and *The Wind Is Rising,* Viola Wendt,
   Carroll College Press
Selected Poems of William Carlos Williams, New Directions
Soup, Robert Newton Peck (in children's library collections)
One Hundred and One Famous Poems, Reilly and Lee
The Imagist Poem, William Pratt, ed., E. P. Dutton
Poetspeak, Paul B. Janeczko, Bradbury Press
Heartland Journal, (biannual for writers over sixty), 3100 Lake
   Mendota Drive, Madison, Wisconsin 53705
The Writer
Writer's Digest
Home Forum, *The Christian Science Monitor*

You will make your own anthologies, especially of essays. Watch
for Melvin Maddocks, Hugh Sidey, Garrison Keillor, and Russell
Baker for examples of tight, good writing.